WELCOME TO

Manage Your Mind

BUILD A BETTER RELATIONSHIP WITH YOUR MIND TODAY

The human mind is complex. We have to manage our thoughts, feelings and emotions on a daily basis, and sometimes this can be overwhelming. Understanding the physical, mental and emotional processes that take place when we feel and behave in certain ways is essential if we want to build a better relationship with our mind and live a happier life. Why do we feel certain emotions in specific situations? Why do we behave in particular ways? And what can we do to overcome the things that hold us back? Learn all this and more by delving into the world of psychology to build a better relationship with your mind.

Contents

6 YOUR MENTAL HEALTH MASTERCLASS

12 DOES YOUR MIND NEED A SERVICE?

14 UNDERSTANDING DEPRESSION

20 HOW SEASONS CAN CHANGE YOUR MOOD

22 INSIDE ANXIETY

28 UNDERSTANDING OVERWHELM

32 WHAT IS BRAIN FOG?

34 BUILDING TO A BURNOUT

38 HOW TO STRESS BETTER

40 PANICKED? PRESS PAUSE

44 COPING WITH PTSD

50 DEALING WITH INTRUSIVE THOUGHTS

54 UNDERSTANDING DISSOCIATIVE DISORDERS

60 LIVING WITH ADHD

66 WHY WE GET ADDICTED

CONTENTS

68 COPING WITH CATASTROPHIC THOUGHTS

70 GRADES OF GRIEF

74 OVERCOMING IMPOSTER SYNDROME

78 FEELING INFERIOR

82 DEVELOP A POSITIVE BODY IMAGE

86 YOU CAN FACE YOUR FEARS

90 THE ART OF LETTING GO

94 BAD HABITS AND HOW TO BREAK THEM

102 MEDITATION AND THE BRAIN

108 MODERN MEDITATION

112 PUT PEN TO PAPER

116 LET THE TREES TREAT YOU

118 EMBRACE THE BLUE

122 COULD COLOUR BE THE CURE?

126 WHICH THERAPY IS FOR ME?

YOUR MENTAL HEALTH MASTERCLASS

YOUR MENTAL HEALTH MASTERCLASS

YOUR MENTAL HEALTH *Masterclass*

We look after our physical health, but our emotional wellbeing often gets neglected. It's time to make it a priority

WORDS NATALIA LUBOMIRSKI

Despite a staggering one in four people in the UK experiencing a mental health problem each year, the invisible nature of it means there's often a tendency to ignore problems and just get on with it. But, as Stephen Buckley, head of information at mental health charity Mind, says, "Mental health is just like our physical health: everybody has it and we need to take care of it."

He adds, "Thankfully, we've seen the national conversation on mental health move forward, but those with mental health problems still face barriers." The topic remains taboo, especially for older »

> "THE INVISIBLE NATURE OF IT MEANS THERE'S A TENDENCY TO IGNORE PROBLEMS"

MANAGE YOUR MIND

generations – a YouGov survey revealed 25% of over-55s think it's more difficult for them to discuss mental health than younger people. Some 71% felt this was because, in the past, anxiety and depression were seen as weaknesses, rather than health conditions.

ROAD TO RECOVERY

These figures are no surprise, especially after the recent pandemic. But it's how we deal with it that's important. Thankfully, there are things we can do. "Eating healthily, sleeping well, exercising and seeking help are all key," says Stephen. "Different treatments work for different people and the journey to recovery won't always be easy."

Here, Mind shares its advice on three common mental health issues.

DEPRESSION

What is it? In its mildest form, it means being repeatedly in low spirits – at its most severe, it can be life-threatening, making you feel suicidal.
The impact? Symptoms can include "feeling low, numb, worthless or without hope," says Stephen. "You may sleep too much or too little, and withdraw from social contact."
Help yourself List activities, people and places that make you feel good, and try to find ways to bring these things into your daily routine.
Do something new This can boost your mood and break unhelpful patterns of thinking. You could try volunteering – it makes you feel better and less alone.
Try self-help Explore cognitive behavioural therapy.

ANXIETY

What is it? Feeling anxious is a natural response when we feel under threat. But if you regularly experience anxiety, including panic attacks, which are strong, last a long time and are difficult to control, you may need help.
The impact? You avoid situations that may make you feel anxious. You'll find it hard to go about your everyday life or do things you enjoy.
Help yourself focus on breathing, especially during a panic attack. Inhale through your nose and out through your mouth, counting from one to five.
Try complementary and alternative therapies, including meditation, aromatherapy, massage, yoga and reflexology, to aid relaxation.
Not sure if you have a problem? Read on to find out more about the secret signs of anxiety.

OBSESSIVE COMPULSIVE DISORDER (OCD)

What is it? An anxiety disorder with obsessions (unwelcome thoughts, urges and worries that appear in your mind, making you feel anxious) and compulsions (repetitive activities to reduce anxiety, such as checking a door is locked or repeating phrases).
The impact? You might avoid situations that trigger it, including work or seeing friends or family. You may feel ashamed of your thoughts or feel the need to hide your OCD.
Help yourself Talk to someone you trust or write down feelings to discuss together.
Learn to relax Manage stress

> **"IT'S THOUGHT THAT AROUND THREE MILLION PEOPLE IN THE UK HAVE AN ANXIETY DISORDER"**

and try techniques such as deep breathing or mindfulness.
Try peer support This brings together people who have had similar experiences. It helps you feel accepted and confident.

NO MORE FEELING ANXIOUS!

Millions of us are experiencing anxiety, often without even realising it. Most of us probably think we know what anxiety feels like. Your heart races, you're short of breath, and your body is bathed in a sheen of sweat. But there are plenty of hidden signs, too. Follow this advice on how to spot the hidden signs and do something about it.

"Anxiety is what we feel when we are worried, tense or afraid," says Nicky Lidbetter, CEO of Anxiety UK. It can be caused by a number of factors, including feelings of uncertainty, physical health problems, stress, and your childhood experiences. It's thought that around three million people in the UK have an anxiety disorder, and while clammy hands and a pounding heart could signal anxiety, some signs are less obvious. Here are the more subtle symptoms to look out for …

YOU OVER-DRAMATISE SMALL FAILURES

"There's a catastrophising nature to anxiety that makes you perceive things being much worse than they actually are," says Nicky. If you're overdramatic, you may have an over-the-top reaction to a small failing, which could lead to a meltdown or cause you to stay at home for the next few days, unable to face the world.

COULD YOU BE SAD?

Does your mood and energy dip in the winter months? SAD is a mood disorder or depression that comes and goes in a seasonal pattern. Symptoms, including a persistent low mood, anxiety, loss of interest in everyday activities, irritability, feeling lethargic, sleeping for longer, craving carbs and gaining weight, are more apparent during winter. What helps? When it comes to SAD, "the same rules apply as to general depression," says Dr Jeff Foster (drjefffoster.co.uk). He suggests exercise, a healthy diet, reducing alcohol intake, socialising and keeping mentally active as ways to reduce symptoms, as well as getting outside as much as you can during daylight hours.

YOUR MENTAL HEALTH MASTERCLASS

WHAT IS STRESS?

Being under pressure is part of life, and it can help you take action, feel energised and get results. But if you are overwhelmed, these feelings could be a problem. While stress isn't a psychiatric diagnosis, it's closely linked to mental health. Manage external pressures and develop your emotional resilience so you're better at coping, including looking after physical health, giving yourself a break and building support networks.

YOU OVERTHINK
"When you're anxious, you're desperately trying to make sense of a situation. Overthinking and labouring over every eventuality is a way of protecting yourself and gaining control," says Nicky.

YOU'RE AFRAID TO TAKE RISKS
Sticking to your 'comfort zone' means you won't have to face frustration, embarrassment, sadness, anger or disappointment – all extreme feelings for someone with anxiety. "When we're anxious, we want to protect ourselves and can see risks as threats, so we become risk-averse," says Nicky.

YOU TALK TOO MUCH
You may be in a 'high-functioning' state when you're anxious, meaning your mind is going at 100mph. As a result, your actions – such as talking a lot – may follow suit. »

YOU'RE CRITICAL OF YOURSELF AND OTHERS
"Being anxious leads to you being hard on yourself. It thrives on the lack of self-esteem you have for yourself and, as a result, you become self-critical and critical of those around you," says Nicky.

YOU CAN'T SLEEP
When we're in an anxious state, it can be hard for our body and mind to relax, and we can have trouble sleeping, which can lead to bouts of insomnia.

YOU'RE DISTRACTED
"We may be preoccupied with our thoughts and easily distracted," says Nicky. Experiencing racing thoughts is common with anxiety, but this attention to the 'inner dialogue' can result in others perceiving us as distant.

> "BEING ANXIOUS THRIVES ON THE LACK OF SELF-ESTEEM YOU HAVE"

MANAGE YOUR MIND

YOUR MENTAL HEALTH MASTERCLASS

"TRYING TO HIDE SYMPTOMS FROM OTHERS CAN IMPACT PHYSICAL HEALTH"

YOU'RE UNWILLING TO MAKE FRIENDS
Opening yourself up emotionally can make you feel vulnerable and exposed. You may already be imagining losing that friendship before it's even started. "Anxiety may isolate us by way of protecting ourselves from unknown territory," says Nicky.

YOU FEEL UNWELL
Constant anxiety has a big effect on the immune system, and trying to hide symptoms from others can impact physical health. "Anxiety can make us fatigued and even sick. Plus, adrenaline released can have a negative impact on our stomachs, as well as other parts of the body," explains Nicky.

When it's more serious...
Seek additional help and support if anxiety is disrupting your day-to-day life and stopping you from doing activities you previously enjoyed.

SHORTCUTS TO SERENITY
These quick tips can help, so make sure you practise them daily:

A person who feels they are not worth listening to will speak quickly, because they don't want to keep others waiting on something not worth listening to. A person in authority speaks slowly; even if you don't feel

MANAGE YOUR MIND

very confident, try slowing down and see how it feels.

Too much to do? Write down each task you can't do right now on a separate piece of paper. Then, every other day, take a random one and do it. You'll soon get through the list.

Learn to recognise negative self-talk ('I can't run any more, I've got to stop'). Visualise it as an irritating bug, stamp on it, kill it, then replace it with a positive one ('Come on, I can do this! Only half a mile left!').

Laugh often. Watch a funny film or a YouTube video and have a good belly laugh. Science shows it helps to lower the stress hormone cortisol and can shift a low mood.

You are what you do, so if you change what you do, you change what you are. Act in a positive way, take action instead of telling yourself you can't. Talk to people in a positive way. You'll soon start to notice a difference.

If you choose to say 'no' to something, mentally rehearse the conversation beforehand, saying it simply and directly, giving no more than one key reason. Do not get into explaining or arguing: just repeat 'No, because…' quietly and firmly.

Before always saying 'yes' to demands, take a deep breath, so you can touch base with yourself to discover what you would truly, honestly prefer to do.

Have a list of useful apps that benefit your mental health. Try Headspace, Stress & Anxiety Companion, and Catch It.

Don't aim too high. Set a goal you know you can achieve, then achieve it. You'll feel good. Now set another and achieve that. Soon you'll be setting bigger goals and achieving those, too.

Visualise yourself at your most confident, then link this feeling to a physical action, such as pinching your thumb and forefinger together. Next time you need to feel confident in a situation, pinch your thumb and finger together to get back to that positive mental state.

Keep talking. Having a chat with a loved one, sending a text to a friend, or asking your colleague to go for a walk is the best tonic for a low mood.

Standing tall and straight makes you feel better about yourself. Imagine a piece of string is pulling the top of your head towards the sky, and the rest of your body straightens accordingly.

Immerse yourself in nature. So-called 'green therapy', being outdoors is a powerful mood-lifter. A Stanford University study showed that a 90-minute walk in nature reduced ruminations, which is a risk factor for mental illness.

HOW TO BE CALM

"If you're feeling anxious, there are ways you can step back and take control before the symptoms build up and take over," says Nicky.

DO A BREATHING EXERCISE
Breathe in through the nose for three seconds, hold for four seconds, breathe out through the mouth slowly for five seconds.

USE A DISTRACTION TECHNIQUE
Try the 5, 4, 3, 2, 1 technique – acknowledge five things you can see, four things you can hear, three things you can touch, two things you can smell, and finally one deep breath in and out.

TRY POSITIVE AFFIRMATIONS
Tell yourself, 'I am safe, I am in control, this feeling is anxiety', and repeat until you feel more in control of your feelings.

MAKE DIETARY CHANGES
Small changes to your diet can make a difference to anxiety symptoms. Try eating less processed food, drinking less alcohol, and cutting back or stopping caffeine. Don't forget that caffeine can be present in chocolate and soft drinks, too.

GET ENOUGH SLEEP
Maintain a regular sleeping pattern by going to bed at the same time each night, switching off screens at least one hour before bedtime, and ensuring your bedroom is dark and the right temperature.

DOES YOUR MIND NEED A SERVICE?

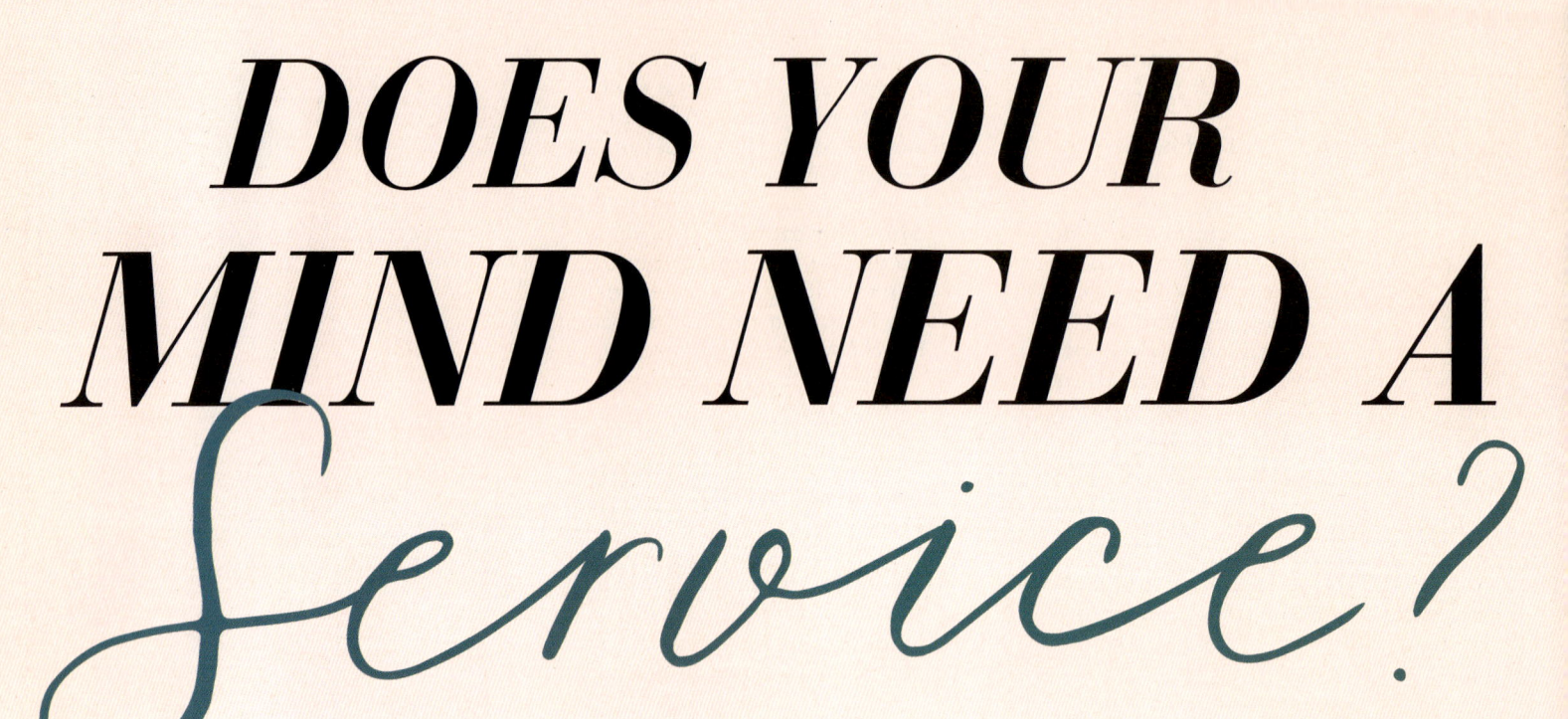

DOES YOUR MIND NEED A *Service?*

If you're feeling out of sorts, discover the tweaks that will get you back on track

WORDS ROSE GOODMAN

Whether you're preoccupied with money worries, your own or your family's health, or you're simply struggling to juggle daily demands, the stresses of life can have a huge impact on your mental and physical health. Not sure what the solution is? Take this quiz to find out how well you're muddling through and try our expert tips to feel more in control.

Take the TEST
Grab a pen and tick the answer that most sounds like you.

1. WHICH OF THE FOLLOWING STATEMENTS MOST ACCURATELY DESCRIBES YOUR SOCIAL LIFE?

- It's lacking, despite my best efforts.
- I'm invited to things but I often cancel at the last minute.
- I struggle to fit plans in with everything else.
- Sometimes it feels like another chore but at the same time I hate missing out.

MANAGE YOUR MIND

DOES YOUR MIND NEED A SERVICE?

AT THE END OF A STRESSFUL DAY, ARE YOU ABLE TO SWITCH OFF?
- 🟪 I just have a glass of wine and go to bed.
- 🟨 Only if I'm able to vent my frustrations to loved ones.
- 🟪 With difficulty – I'm always worrying about something.
- 🟦 No, I find it hard to keep things in perspective when under pressure.

A FAMILY MEMBER IS UNWELL, YOUR WORKLOAD IS HUGE AND THE HOUSE IS A MESS. HOW DO YOU COPE?
- 🟨 Take on everything myself.
- 🟦 I'm spinning the plates, but feel overwhelmed.
- 🟪 I bury my head in the sand.
- 🟪 I'm on the brink of burnout.

HOW WOULD YOU BEST DESCRIBE YOUR MOOD RECENTLY?
- 🟦 Panicked and restless.
- 🟨 Positive with the odd wobble.
- 🟪 Tense and impatient.
- 🟪 Running on autopilot without much feeling.

WHEN YOU LOOK AT YOUR DIARY FOR THE WEEK, HOW DO YOU FEEL?
- 🟪 Dread at having to fake enthusiasm for others.
- 🟦 What diary? I'm not that organised.
- 🟨 Prepared, but I wish I had more fun social plans.
- 🟪 Exhausted and it hasn't even started.

WHERE DOES YOUR MIND WANDER TO WHEN YOU'RE FEELING OVERWHELMED?
- 🟪 A dark room and no disruptions.
- 🟨 Dinner with loved ones.
- 🟪 A desert island, far away.
- 🟦 There's no time for my mind to wander!

WOULD YOU SAY YOU ARE EATING WELL AND EXERCISING?
- 🟪 I often don't have the energy.
- 🟪 For the most part – it helps me focus.
- 🟦 I eat on the go but struggle to fit in a workout.
- 🟨 No – food and binge-watching TV are my comforts.

YOUR RESULTS

MOSTLY BLUE
YOU NEED ROUTINE
Life is feeling chaotic

"Establishing and maintaining a routine can give you a sense of stability, predictability and a certain level of control. This not only reduces anxiety and stress, but can also improve focus and productivity," says therapist Marisa Peer.

Try...
Setting a realistic plan. But be honest about the energy you can commit daily, says Marisa. Overly ambitious goals will lead to frustration if you're unable to stick to them. For example, aim to wake up at a time each day that allows you to ease into the morning – whether that's with a coffee or a brisk walk – then gradually add in other nourishing activities. Download Todoist to stay on track, a free app from the App Store and Google Play.

MOSTLY PINK
YOU NEED CONNECTION
You're craving quality time with loved ones but it falls off the radar with life's demands

This lack of connection, over time, can lead to loneliness and depression[1]. "As social creatures, our brains are wired for interaction," says Dr Touroni. It can help to reduce anxiety and improve self-esteem.

Try...
Reaching out. It might feel difficult at first, especially if you struggle to ask for help, but it will quickly become a trained muscle. Make a promise to yourself to contact at least one person each week for a catch-up. Sharing diaries with friends can also be a great way to schedule physical time together so you have something to look forward to. And don't cancel – unless there's an emergency!

MOSTLY YELLOW
YOU NEED DOWNTIME
Even when you're sleeping, you're unable to fully switch off

It's a recipe not only for mental exhaustion, but for weakening your immune system[2]. "Too much output without replenishing can lead to burnout," says consultant psychologist Dr Elena Touroni[3].

Try...
Scheduling in some rest time. This doesn't need to be a full day of reclining on the sofa. "Small chunks of self-care can help refill your 'energy bank'," says Dr Touroni. "The important thing is finding what best works for you – whether that's a quick yoga session or reading a chapter of your favourite book." And make it non-negotiable – write it in your diary just like you would any other commitment.

MOSTLY PURPLE
YOU NEED AN OUTLET
All work and no play can cause your mental health to crash

"Engaging in activities you love provides a source of comfort and distraction," says Marisa. They are also a great natural way to boost those feel-good hormones dopamine and serotonin.

Try...
Finding what makes you happy. Instead of 'zoning out' on devices or watching TV, think about what you used to enjoy as a child. Arts and craft? Spending time with animals? We often lose touch with this playful side as adults, but hobbies can help to reduce stress and even protect our heart health[4]. Search 'groups' on Facebook to discover what your local community has to offer, and consider volunteering as an option.

MANAGE YOUR MIND

[1] Massachusetts General Hospital. [2] PLoS One. [3] Co-founder of The Chelsea Psychology Clinic. [4] Psychosomatic Medicine.

Understanding DEPRESSION

We explore the symptoms, causes, risk factors and treatment options for one of the most common mental health conditions in the world

WORDS JULIE BASSETT

Depression is one of the most common mental health disorders. There's a good chance you have experienced depression, either yourself, a loved one or a friend. According to the World Health Organization, depressive disorder (as depression is also known) affects 3.8% of the world's population, including 5% of adults. That's around 280 million people who have depression globally, and it's more common in women than men. Yet, despite this, not everyone accesses treatment, whether that's due to social stigma, overburdened services, or a lack of mental health training. It's talked about more openly now than it has been in the past, but it's still a misunderstood condition.

Depression is a disorder that has a negative impact on how you think, feel, act or perceive the world around you. Everyone gets down, or has periods of sadness or low mood, but usually these pass, whether this is due to the removal of the trigger causing the sadness or because mood naturally lifts over time. However, in a depressive disorder, the symptoms are felt for long periods of time, ie most of the day, consistently every day for many weeks. Two weeks without improvement in symptoms is usually the point at which depression is considered as a diagnosis.

Signs and symptoms

Generally speaking, depression makes you feel sad, low, hopeless and not interested in things that you usually enjoy. This can have a huge impact on your life, your hobbies, your work and your relationships. Specific symptoms can vary from person to person, but there are some common psychological changes in the way you think and feel. You might experience low self-esteem, feel irritable, lack motivation, be unable to make decisions, lack any enjoyment in life, have anxiety or intense worry, suffer from guilt, or be more tearful than usual. If depression is severe or untreated, some people may start to have thoughts of self-harm or suicide, which is why it's so important to seek help for yourself or a loved one as soon as symptoms are recognised. Symptoms can stretch into other parts of your life as well, meaning that you avoid contact with friends, stop attending social events, and avoid activities, interests and sports.

While it is a mental health condition, there are sometimes accompanying physical symptoms too, such as changes to your appetite, sleep, sex drive and energy levels.

Depression can appear to come out of nowhere, but it usually happens gradually. It can start with feeling more sad than usual, not wanting to go out, or feeling tearful, which can then happen more and more often, and you may begin to withdraw from life. It can be hard to recognise in yourself, particularly if you've never experienced it before, and often it's someone else in our lives who notices, such as a colleague, friend or family member. Even then, it can be difficult to broach the subject; we're not all well educated in mental health conditions and how to have those conversations.

It's a complex condition that affects each individual in its own way, and while there are common symptoms, there are also sometimes other reasons for those symptoms. For example, those who are struggling with grief after a bereavement can experience many of the same symptoms, as a natural response to the loss (though grief can also lead to depression). Some conditions can be misdiagnosed as depression due to similarities in some symptoms, such as anxiety (though they can also occur together, or can cause each other), ADHD, chronic fatigue syndrome, fibromyalgia, hypothyroidism or post-traumatic stress disorder. It's important to get an accurate diagnosis, as this can help with accessing the right treatment options. »

> "Depression can have a huge impact on your life, hobbies, work and relationships"

UNDERSTANDING DEPRESSION

MANAGE YOUR MIND 15

Severity and types of depression

There are different types of depression, ranging from mild to severe, which is determined by the type, severity and frequency of symptoms, how long it's been going on for, and the impact that it's having on everyday life.

The most common form of depression is often called 'clinical depression' or 'major depression' and is usually what is meant by the term 'depression' on its own without any other modifiers. This is moderate to severe depression that lasts more than two weeks and usually requires some form of therapy and/or medication to help treat it. This is usually diagnosed by the presence of the classic depression symptoms as well as the length of time you've had it for.

Dysthymia (known as persistent depressive disorder or PDD) is a milder but longer-term form of depression. This is a low mood that lasts for at least two years, but it usually has less severe symptoms than major depression. It can have less of an impact on your day-to-day activities, but you may feel sad or lacking joy most of the time. Sometimes this can develop into major depression at times, which is why it's key to get early treatment in place to help prevent a worsening of the condition.

Other types of depression can be caused by specific triggers. In the case of seasonal affective disorder (SAD), depressive episodes are triggered by the change in seasons from summer to autumn and winter. It's usually linked to the shorter days and longer periods of darkness, so treatment can include light therapy, as well as the more traditional depression treatments.

Postnatal depression is a specific form of depression that happens after having a baby, either immediately or in the 12 months following the birth. It's relatively common, with statistics from the NHS (UK) suggesting it impacts one in ten women in the first year after childbirth. The symptoms are the same as major depression, and it can be more likely to happen if someone has a history of mental health problems, including previous depressive periods, as well as a lack of support or after experiencing traumatic events. Postnatal depression can affect fathers and partners too, and it's also possible to get antenatal depression during the pregnancy. Linked to the reproductive system is premenstrual dysphoric disorder (PMDD), which is a more severe type of premenstrual syndrome (PMS) in which a woman has symptoms of depression and anxiety for a week or two before their period.

Then there is bipolar disorder, which can sometimes be called 'manic depression'. In this case, a person will swing from severe depression to an excessively high mood ('mania'), both states of which can have a huge impact on a person's life, and treatment is required to help stabilise a person's condition. Classic major depression is sometimes called 'unipolar depression' to differentiate from bipolar disorder, as it doesn't involve periods of mania.

Causes and risk factors for depression

We don't yet fully understand what causes depression, as it's a complex condition and there are usually multiple risk factors involved in each case. There may be a specific trigger, something happening in your life that negatively impacts on your mental health. Other factors can include loneliness, long periods of stress, loss, lack of social interactions or not getting enough sleep. Stressful life events are often behind cases of depression, such as a bereavement or the end of a relationship. Depression can also be caused by things like pregnancy and giving birth, as well as menopause and the years leading up to it (while menopause can cause mood swings and sadness, it's not always depression, though the transition can trigger a period of depression as well). Depression can also be triggered by substance use, such as drinking too much alcohol or taking drugs. A University of Bristol report from 2022 showed that smoking can increase the risk of developing depression between 54% and 132% – of the six million smokers in England alone, 1.6 million are estimated to have depression and/or anxiety. Illness can also be a trigger for depression, particularly chronic, long-term illnesses or serious conditions such as coronary heart disease or cancer.

There is a theory that depression might be a defence mechanism by the body, causing it to shut down and preserve energy in response to a perceived threat, but the research is lacking in proving the theory at this time. There are also studies looking at whether diet can have an impact; one systemic review study[1] concluded that, 'there may be a significant connection between certain dietary behaviours and signs and symptoms of depression in people of all ages'. It found that avoiding ultra-processed junk food and fast food, and eating more fruits and vegetables, may lower the risk of developing depressive symptoms. There is also some (limited) evidence that eating Omega-3 fatty acids can be protective against developing depression.

Another significant factor is family history and genetics. Having a history of depression in your family doesn't mean that you will definitely experience it yourself, but it is a risk factor and can make it more likely. An article published by Stanford Medicine called 'Major Depression and Genetics' suggests that heritability is around 40-50%, meaning that for those who suffer from depression it could be attributed 50% to genetics and 50% to

Are some people more likely to have depression?

Some personality types and traits can indicate that a person is more likely to suffer from depression; those who are more prone to engaging in other forms of negative thinking are more likely to develop depression. For example, if someone tends to catastrophise, spend a lot of time going over events or conversations, have low self-esteem, or struggle with negative self-talk, this can potentially trigger a depressive episode. People who fall under the 'neuroticism' personality trait may be associated with a higher risk of depression and anxiety, as this trait indicates a person has trouble with negative emotions, self-regulation, difficulty managing stress, and a tendency to complain. There are also links between perfectionism and the risk of developing depression.

Introversion can also be a risk factor for depression, as introverts can sometimes keep their thoughts internal and spend more time ruminating on them. They may feel less comfortable talking about what they're feeling. While introversion can also mean that people are more in tune with their thoughts, and therefore may be more aware of a negative pattern emerging, it can mean that when something goes wrong – ie an external stress factor – an introverted person can turn inwards and not seek social support. One comparative study[2] found that, 'The overall level of neuroticism is markedly and introversion somewhat higher in depressive patients than in the general population'.

Around the world, women are 1.7 times more likely to have depression than men, says one research study[3]. Up until puberty, boys and girls have similar rates of depression, but from ages 14 to 25 years the ratio between young women and men is at its highest at almost double the risk, with the ratio decreasing again with age and prevalence becoming similar again from age 65 years onwards. In the same study, the author writes that the fact depression can be associated with puberty, the menstrual cycle, pregnancy and menopause suggests female hormonal fluctuations may be a trigger for depression, though there is a distinct lack of studies that focus on sex-specific mechanisms behind depression.

Medical and therapeutic interventions

It can be hard to seek help for depression. For a start, it can be difficult to recognise that that's what it is, and then it can also be difficult to know where to go for help. It's usually best to speak to your regular doctor first, who can signpost you to the relevant treatment options and resources. While women are more likely to suffer from depression, they are also more likely to seek help than men, and there are specific services and online websites dedicated to helping men to come forward for support. Depression can lift by itself with no intervention, but this can take weeks or months, and leave a long-term impact. Untreated depression can also be more likely to come back in the future, and may be more severe when it comes back. In cases of mild depression, a 'wait and see' approach can be taken, but usually for a short period of time to see if it lifts, otherwise treatment is recommended.

The two main routes for treatment include medication and therapy, with both as effective as each other in isolation, but a mix of the two is often the best course of action. This can be combined with lifestyle changes and self-care to help prevent the risk of future depressive episodes and to aid in recovery.

For moderate to severe depression, medication can help, usually in the form of antidepressants. Antidepressants act on neurotransmitters in the brain to help relieve the symptoms of depression. The most commonly prescribed type are SSRIs (selective serotonin reuptake inhibitors), which can help the brain to create new nerve connections and inhibit certain neurotransmitters. It can take time for these kinds of drugs to kick in, and symptoms can occasionally worsen for a short period at first, but from about six to eight weeks, improvements should be noticed. Antidepressants shouldn't be stopped suddenly either, and it's recommended to stay on them for many months after symptoms have improved, before tapering the dose off. Many people are reluctant to take medication, but it can be a really big help in symptom relief, freeing you up to work on other treatments to tackle the underlying causes and be motivated enough for lifestyle interventions, such as increased exercise.

Therapies can include self-help guided therapy, which involves working through an online or physical set of resources, based on CBT (cognitive behavioural

HOW TO SPEAK TO A FRIEND IN NEED

If you notice the signs and symptoms of depression in someone close to you, you might feel a bit lost when it comes to offering help. Some people aren't ready to seek help, so it's important not to put any pressure on them. But you can let them know that you're worried about them, ask them if they need any support, let them know that there is help available when they want it, and be open about depression so that it isn't a taboo subject. They may not want to meet up or talk about it, but sometimes a quick text to say you're thinking of them can be very appreciated. You may be able to help in a more practical way, providing a meal, helping with housework or walking the dog, for example. And when they're ready to seek support, you can be there for them throughout the process so they're not going through it alone.

> **"THERE ARE SPECIFIC SERVICES AND ONLINE WEBSITES DEDICATED TO HELPING MEN"**

Q&A: CBT AND WHY IT'S EFFECTIVE

ANJALI MEHTA CHANDAR
CLINICAL DIRECTOR OF BRIGHTER LIFE THERAPY

Anjali is a CBT therapist, lecturer and clinical director of Brighter Life Therapy, an award-winning private counselling practice offering CBT and psychotherapy for children and adults with anxiety, depression and stress.

WWW.BRIGHTERLIFETHERAPY.CO.UK
@brighterlifetherapyuk
(Facebook and Instagram)

Can you give us a brief overview of CBT?
CBT stands for 'cognitive behavioural therapy', and is a style of talking therapy, whereby you learn to notice and change unhelpful thoughts and behaviours to impact your mood and the associated uncomfortable physical sensations.

Why is CBT considered an effective form of treatment for depression?
CBT has an amazing evidence base behind it; that means that lots of high-quality research shows it to be an effective treatment for depression. This is why it's routinely offered by the NHS, and many therapists are trained to deliver CBT. You can access CBT through the NHS, your health insurance provider or by paying privately. CBT for depression works by noticing when we're engaging in unhelpful behaviours that keep our low mood going, such as avoiding going out, staying in bed, and not seeing friends or family. It helps us to gradually build our motivation back up, so we can engage in meaningful activities that will boost our mood. CBT for depression will also help clients notice their overly negative thoughts that are perhaps unfair, and we test out how true these really are. This can lead us to generate alternative, more balanced thoughts.

What is the difference between CBT, and other forms of talking therapies like counselling or psychotherapy?
All types of psychotherapy include some level of exploring how the person is feeling, thinking and behaving, and how this may be impacting on their wellbeing. We sometimes refer to CBT as more of a 'doing therapy', as it's not just the talking or exploring element. We utilise a range of techniques for clients to implement outside of sessions to better cope with their difficult feelings and to improve their wellbeing.
CBT is right for someone if they're willing to commit to practice of the interventions outside of sessions. CBT cannot be done to someone; rather it is an active process on behalf of the client – they need to engage with the techniques to see a real relief. This can be hard to do, but it gets easier with more practice, and the therapist is always there to help the client problem solve any issues.
CBT is also really structured, and CBT therapists follow specific protocol(s) designed to target the depression. If someone prefers to spend the therapy hour discussing current events in their life, a counselling approach may suit them better. CBT is also based more in the 'here and now' (although some events from the past are acknowledged in sessions); other psychotherapies may spend more time looking at the past.

At what point should those with depression be considering accessing CBT and how long a commitment is recommended for optimum results?
Early intervention is key! The quicker we can access support, the easier depression is to overcome. Guidelines suggest a 'watchful waiting' period of two weeks of first noticing symptoms of depression to see if things naturally improve. If symptoms do not naturally improve in a few weeks, seek support – you can either reach out to your local NHS Talking Therapies service directly (if in the UK), your doctor, your private health insurer to see if they can offer support on your package, or do an internet search for a local private CBT therapist (just make sure they are BABCP-accredited if in the UK). If symptoms are mild, you may only need six to eight weekly or fortnightly treatment sessions. If your symptoms are more moderate to severe, you may need eight to 16 weekly sessions, or more.

Are there any types of people who CBT is particularly effective for?
CBT is particularly effective for those who are able to commit to weekly/fortnightly sessions, have an open mind to trying different techniques, and engage with these outside of session. For some people, a combined treatment of medication and CBT can also be effective. The medication tends to take the edge off the symptoms so clients can engage with the principles and strategies of CBT, giving them long-term solutions for managing their wellbeing.

therapy) principles. There are also talking therapies, such as counselling or CBT, which you can be referred to via your doctor or you can often self-refer. CBT is one of the most common routes that people take, helping you to understand your thoughts and behaviours – see our expert box to the left for more on this.

Self-care and lifestyle
Lifestyle changes can help to lower the risk of depression, lower the chance of a recurrence of depression, and help with the recovery from depression.

Chief among lifestyle interventions is exercise, which has been repeatedly shown in studies to have a massively positive effect on mental health. One such research paper[4] analysed more than 200 unique studies to identify the optimal dose and type of exercise for treating major depressive disorder, compared to psychotherapy and antidepressants. It found that exercise was an effective, well-tolerated treatment for depression, equally useful for people with and without underlying health conditions. The research found that the most effective forms of exercise were walking or jogging, yoga and strength training, particularly when done intensely, but any movement will have an impact. It concluded that the effects were comparable to medical and therapeutic interventions, and could be used in combination with traditional treatments. In fact, social prescribing is on the rise in both the UK and USA, which connects people to non-clinical resources that can help with depression. This can support those with mental health conditions to find and attend local groups or activities as part of their recovery.

It's not just exercise that can be a great lifestyle intervention. For those without a strong social network, volunteering can give a sense of purpose, which can help with recovery from depression. Similarly, community projects, gardening groups, arts and crafts, and talking support groups can all be effective.

A balanced, healthy diet and a good sleep routine can also have a big impact on the risk of and recovery from depression, as can having a good day-to-day routine, balanced between meaningful work and time spent on hobbies and interests.

There is a branch of social prescribing that is linked to 'green' activities, which supports people to engage in nature. According to mental health support service Mind (mind.org.uk), 'Spending time in green space or bringing nature into your everyday life can benefit both your mental and physical wellbeing'. This could be through things like gardening, growing food, walking or being around animals. Combining these lifestyle interventions can be hugely effective, for example joining an outdoor walking group ticks off exercise, company and nature in one go. Plus, by attending groups or clubs regularly, it can help to build a purposeful routine in life, which is a key element in the journey towards recovery.

There are other self-care tools that can help with depression, such as keeping a mood diary to keep track of potential triggers and themes when you're feeling low, or writing in a journal as an outlet for your thoughts and feelings. Talking is also important, as it can stop negative thoughts from spiralling and enables us to seek advice from others and gain perspective. Some people find that being creative helps with depressive symptoms, while others find that trying new things can break habits and thought patterns.

Slow and steady
Experiencing depression can be overwhelming and taking that move toward help and recovery is intimidating. It can feel like such a big step, and the treatment itself can be difficult and emotional. Trying to remember to take pills, attend therapy sessions, exercise more, get outside, do your hobbies and get quality sleep, while cooking healthy meals and drinking enough water, is enough to create more stress if you try to do it all at once.

It's important to be realistic in recovery and take small steps. There's this societal

> **"SOME PEOPLE FIND THAT BEING CREATIVE HELPS WITH DEPRESSIVE SYMPTOMS"**

pressure to 'bounce back', or to think that life can suddenly return to normal after being prescribed medication, but rushing the process means not dealing with the problems that may have contributed to depression in the first place. There is no quick fix, and it can mean making a commitment to work on yourself for weeks, months and even years.

Unfortunately, depression is a condition that's here to stay, and it's continuing to affect more and more people every year, including younger children. By engaging in whole-life changes to support your physical and mental wellbeing, you're already taking great strides towards lowering your risk of a first or recurrent depression. Be mindful of your thoughts and emotions, so you're more in tune with yourself and able to notice when you're feeling off. The sooner you seek help and treatment, the sooner you can begin your path of recovery should depression impact you.

HOW SEASONS CAN CHANGE YOUR MOOD

HOW *Seasons* CAN CHANGE YOUR MOOD

The science behind seasonal affective disorder and how the brain responds to daylight

WORDS SCOTT DUTFIELD

Often known as winter depression, seasonal affective disorder (SAD) is a form of depression brought about by the changing pattern of the seasons. Typically starting in autumn and lasting throughout winter, many people who suffer from SAD experience symptoms such as feeling lethargic, despair and a general loss of interest in everyday activities. Why some people experience SAD and others don't remains largely a mystery. However, there are many theories, including the seasons throwing your body clock out of sync. Known as circadian rhythm, the body generally follows a sleep-wake cycle across 24 hours that's attuned to the body's exposure to natural sunlight. Increasing light levels at dawn fire up the brain's production of the feel-good hormone serotonin, while decreased light levels at dusk slow serotonin production,

MANAGE YOUR MIND

and in its place starts the production of the sleepy hormone melatonin.

During winter, when light levels during the daytime are lowest, serotonin production is also at its lowest, while melatonin continues to be released. For some, this can leave them longing for summer and feeling symptoms of SAD. However, SAD isn't strictly associated with the darker winter months. During the bright, warm weather of summer and spring, excessive daylight can lead to the reduction of melatonin production to the point where normal sleep is impacted, which can also lead to symptoms of SAD.

Studies of families and twins have found that there may be a hereditary explanation for the expression of SAD. From the differences in genes involved in the transport of serotonin to those keeping circadian rhythm in check, scientists have suggested that SAD may be caused by changes in our DNA. One study by the University of South Wales found that people with blue eyes were less likely to experience SAD compared to those with brown eyes. While the scientists say more research is needed to explain their findings, it's possible that blue eyes are more sensitive to light and have a different threshold to brown eyes for the release of melatonin during the daytime.

SEASONAL GENES

SAD isn't the only way the seasons can alter the way our bodies work. In 2015, a team of international scientists discovered that the seasons could change human genes, especially those involved with immunity and inflammation. Having taken samples of blood and tissue from 16,000 people from around the globe, the researchers found that during December to February for those living north of the equator, and June to August for those south of the equator, genes associated with the body's immune system were more active compared to other seasons. However, among those who live in warm climates near the equator, which experience little seasonal change, the same genes were more active during rainy seasons.

> "SCIENTISTS HAVE SUGGESTED THAT SAD MAY BE CAUSED BY CHANGES IN OUR DNA"

LIGHT THERAPY

Since the 1980s, one of the most widely used treatments to tackle SAD is light therapy. Using a device called a light box, sufferers of SAD sit in front of artificial light, typically in the morning, to stimulate the production of serotonin and reduce the production of melatonin. Unlike other lamps, like those used for tanning, these light boxes come with filters to remove harmful ultraviolet light that can damage the skin and eyes. Some studies have shown that between 30 and 45 minutes of regular exposure to a light box at around 10,000 lux, which is around the intensity of light the sun provides in the morning, is effective in treating SAD. Sufferers may experience some side effects, such as headaches or skin irritation during use, so it's advised to always seek medical advice before using a light box.

MAKING MELATONIN

How the brain uses light to signal the release of this sleep hormone

1 SIGNAL TO THE PACEMAKER
Light enters the eye and triggers a signal from the brain's pacemaker, called the suprachiasmatic nucleus.

2 SENDING A SIGNAL
The signal then travels along nerves via a collection of neurons called the superior cervical ganglia to the pineal gland.

3 HORMONE RELEASE
Once at the pineal gland, the signal stimulates the organ to release a hormone called melatonin.

4 MELATONIN
This hormone acts as the body's natural sedative and encourages the body to fall asleep.

5 OVERPRODUCTION
When the production of melatonin is out of sync with the body's sleep-wake cycle, the effects of SAD are felt.

6 LIGHT
During the daytime, the brain triggers the release of serotonin. However, under low light that shifts to trigger the release of melatonin.

INSIDE Anxiety

The brain's natural fear response evolved to keep our species safe, so what happens when it goes wrong?

WORDS LAURA MEARS

The word anxiety comes from the Latin 'angere', which literally means 'to choke'. It describes the feeling of physical and emotional unease we experience when anticipating a threat. It has been critical to our success as a species, making us feel uncomfortable in the face of danger for thousands of years.

The purpose of anxiety is adaptation. It prepares us to fight or flee if possible, or freeze in place if not. It initiates rapid activation of the sympathetic nervous system, a network of nerves that reach into every corner of the body. These nerves spit out a chemical called noradrenaline, also known as norepinephrine. Related to adrenaline, this chemical initiates a wave of changes that prepare the mind and body for physical action. The heart rate rises, the breathing quickens, the blood vessels in the muscles dilate, and the mind becomes hyper alert.

Researchers disagree about whether anxiety and fear are the same. They both alert us to danger and trigger similar protective biological responses. But, while the focus of fear is often external danger, the focus of anxiety can be anything, physical or psychological, real or hypothetical. In times of physical danger, the changes the fight or flight response triggers are essential. But, often in the case of anxiety, the source of the threat is less tangible.

When there is nothing to fight against or flee from, the physical fear reaction can feel very unpleasant. Side effects include nausea, tingling, dizziness, hot flushes, restlessness, trouble concentrating, irritability, and a feeling often described as an unshakeable sense of dread.

Anxiety disorders

One in four people experience cycles of anxious thoughts and feelings that become so intense that they start to impact their everyday lives. This is when normal human »

> ❝ SIDE EFFECTS INCLUDE NAUSEA, DIZZINESS, HOT FLUSHES AND IRRITABILITY ❞

ANXIETY

INSIDE ANXIETY

THE ANXIETY RESPONSE

Ⓐ CORTEX
The brain's information-processing areas trigger anxious feelings, consciously or subconsciously.

AMYGDALA
The fear centre senses danger and initiates the fight or flight response.

LATERAL PERIAQUEDUCTAL GRAY
The amygdala sends signals to the lateral periaqueductal gray, which tells the muscles to prepare for action.

HYPOTHALAMUS
The amygdala contacts the hypothalamus, telling it to switch on the sympathetic nervous system.

PITUITARY GLAND
The hypothalamus sends chemical messages to the pituitary gland, which starts pumping hormones into the blood.

ADRENAL GLANDS
Hormones from the pituitary gland arrive at the adrenal glands, telling them to make the stress hormone cortisol.

SYMPATHETIC NERVOUS SYSTEM
The sympathetic nervous system releases noradrenaline, and the adrenal glands release adrenaline, two major fight or flight chemicals.

Ⓑ HEART AND LUNGS
The body responds by increasing the heart rate, quickening the breathing, and diverting blood to the muscles.

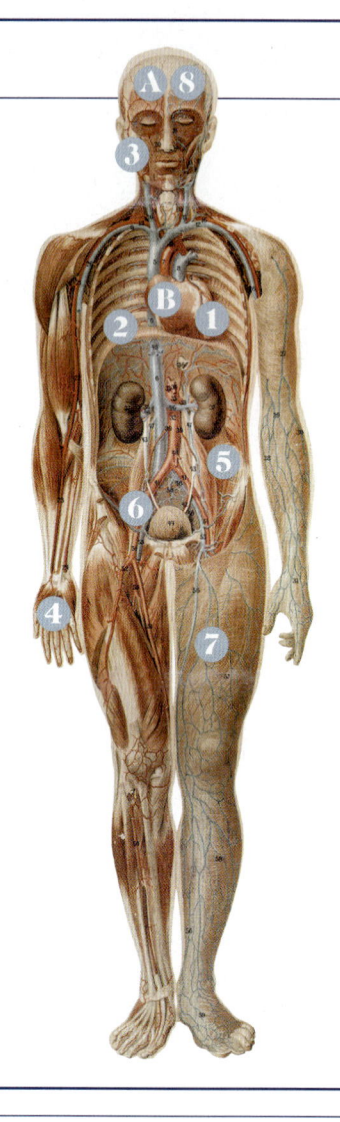

THE EFFECTS OF ANXIETY

① PALPITATIONS
Adrenaline ramps up the heart rate, causing the heart to pound or flutter in the chest.

② BREATHLESSNESS
The muscles scream for oxygen as the body prepares to fight or flee, causing a sensation of breathlessness.

③ HOT FLUSHES
The blood vessels widen to deliver more oxygen to the muscles, making the skin feel hot.

④ SWEATING
The nervous system triggers sweating in the hands, feet, face and armpits.

⑤ NAUSEA
Blood moves away from the intestines and the muscles slow down causing cramping and nausea.

⑥ DIARRHOEA
Contractions in the large intestine speed up to empty the bowel.

⑦ TREMBLING
The muscles prepare to jump into action, and become twitchy and overexcited.

⑧ PANIC
The physical symptoms feed back to the brain, magnifying feelings of restlessness and panic.

WHAT CAUSES PANIC ATTACKS?

Panic attacks can start without warning, flooding the body with a wave of physical symptoms that seem to have come from nowhere. But these events don't happen totally out of the blue. Researchers at Southern Methodist University have shown that signs of an impending panic attack can begin up to an hour beforehand. Monitoring people with panic disorder revealed that, in the run-up to a panic attack, blood carbon dioxide levels start to fall. Then, just before the panic attack begins, they suddenly rise. This makes the brain think that it is suffocating, triggering feelings of intense fear. The link between carbon dioxide and panic attacks might explain why slow, deep breathing is such an effective treatment. It helps to restore the body back to its normal balance.

anxiety becomes an anxiety disorder. This group of psychiatric conditions can be acute or chronic, lasting a short amount of time or persisting for years. There are many types, ranging from generalised anxiety and panic attacks to phobias and obsessive compulsive disorder.

Doctors have known about anxiety disorders for centuries. The father of medicine, Hippocrates, described a man called Nicanor, who had a phobia of the flute more than 2,000 years ago. Hearing the sound of the instrument would cause him intense anxiety. At the time, there was no diagnosis and no treatment. Clinical understanding of anxiety has improved dramatically over the centuries, but it wasn't until relatively recently that the biology of fear, panic and anxiety started to become clear.

One of the first researchers to investigate anxiety was Ivan Pavlov. The physiologist noticed strange behaviour in his animals after a traumatic event. In September 1924, a storm flooded St Petersburg. Pavlov's dog kennels were submerged. To escape the rising water, the dogs had to swim to the laboratory on

> **RECENTLY, THE BIOLOGY OF FEAR, PANIC AND ANXIETY BECAME CLEAR**

the floor above. They endured terrifying sights and sounds on their journey, including lashing rain, crashing waves and falling trees.

After the storm subsided, some dogs returned to their training as though nothing had happened. But others became troubled and withdrawn. Writing about one of the dogs, Pavlov explained, "the animal was abnormally restless and all conditioned reflexes were practically absent… the animal now would not touch the food". This dog was experiencing post-traumatic stress disorder. All the staff could do to reassure it and restore its normal behaviour was to keep it company.

Why only some of the dogs developed anxiety after the flood is a big question in anxiety research. Individuals can experience the same life events and emerge with completely different psychological reactions; they seem to have their own thresholds for anxiety disorder development. It is likely that these thresholds are influenced by genetics.

Genetic causes

The centre of the brain's fear response is a pair of walnut-sized structures called the amygdala. This cellular junction box communicates across the brain. It receives inputs from the sensory system, keeping a constant watch for signs of danger. If it detects a problem, it sends signals to the hypothalamus and the brain stem, which activate the fight or flight response.

One of the brain areas that sends signals into the amygdala is a group of cells called the raphe nuclei. These cells send out the feel-good brain chemical serotonin. This chemical has gained a reputation for being the 'happy hormone', but its role in anxiety is not so positive.

A group of antidepressants called selective serotonin reuptake inhibitors (SSRIs) help to improve mood by keeping serotonin around in the brain for longer, but they can also increase anxiety. Researchers at the University of North Carolina Healthcare wanted to understand why, so they tracked the activity of serotonin nerves in the brains of mice. They traced serotonin-induced anxiety back to a group of cells that connect the raphe nuclei to a brain area called the 'bed nucleus of the stria terminalis'. »

TYPES OF ANXIETY

GENERALISED ANXIETY DISORDER
This common form of anxiety has no specific trigger. People experience uncontrollable worry about a variety of aspects of life, from work to relationships.

PANIC DISORDER
People with panic disorder experience regular sudden panic attacks. The frequency can range from a few times a month to more than once a week.

SOCIAL ANXIETY DISORDER
People with social anxiety experience overwhelming worry before, during or after interacting with other people. It is sometimes known as social phobia.

POST-TRAUMATIC STRESS DISORDER
This type of anxiety, often abbreviated to PTSD, is most often triggered by a traumatic life event. Symptoms include flashbacks, nightmares and extreme alertness to danger.

PHOBIA
A phobia is an overactive fear response to something specific, like an object, a situation or a bodily sensation. Even thinking about the subject of the phobia can trigger anxiety.

OBSESSIVE COMPULSIVE DISORDER
Also known as OCD, this type of anxiety has two key features. First, frequent unwanted (obsessive) thoughts. Second, repetitive (compulsive) behaviours that help to relieve the thoughts.

HEALTH ANXIETY
This type of anxiety focuses on bodily health, with intense worry about being or becoming unwell. The physical sensations of anxiety itself can make these worries worse.

Sometimes known as the 'extended amygdala', this brain area links the parts of the brain that sense danger with the parts of the brain that trigger a response. Serotonin signals here change the messages that reach the brain's fight or flight switchboard, the hypothalamus. When serotonin levels increase, the hypothalamus flips the parasympathetic nervous system 'off', and the sympathetic nervous system 'on'. This causes anxiety to rise.

Changes to the serotonin signalling system appear frequently in studies searching for the genetic causes of anxiety. Researchers have identified mutations in several serotonin-related genes that appear to increase the risk of anxiety disorders. These include the genes for the receptor that detects serotonin, the transporter that clears it away, and the enzyme that breaks it down.

Some individuals with these genetic changes even have visible differences inside their brains. Scans have shown that genetic differences in serotonin signalling can alter the connections between the amygdala and a part of the brain called the fusiform gyrus, which is responsible for face detection.

Another group of brain chemicals that play a role in anxiety are the catecholamines. These include the fight or flight chemicals adrenaline and noradrenaline (also known as epinephrine and norepinephrine). Nerves that make noradrenaline start in a part of the brain called the locus coeruleus, or 'blue spot', which communicates with the amygdala. It has a powerful role to play in vigilance and attention, and it helps to tune incoming sensory signals.

Nerve impulses from the locus coeruleus dial up the amygdala's fear response. They instruct the fear centre to send messages to the hypothalamus that tell it to release a chemical called corticotropin-releasing hormone. This tells the brain's pituitary gland to release a hormone that prepares the body for incoming stress. Researchers at Boston Children's Hospital found that blocking corticotropin-releasing hormone makes cautious mice fearless. They visit brightly lit areas, walk across narrow planks, and don't hesitate to investigate strange new objects.

Environmental factors

Not everyone with alterations in their genetic makeup will go on to develop anxiety. Genetics might determine a person's underlying threshold for developing a particular anxiety disorder, but life events determine whether that threshold will ever be breached.

Research has shown that anxiety disorders rarely occur on their own. In fact, 60-90% of people with anxiety also have another mental health condition. This might be depression, substance misuse or another

COPING WITH ANXIETY

Take these simple steps to sooth a mind in overdrive:

SORT YOUR THOUGHTS
Are your worries practical? If so, plan to do something about them. Are they hypothetical? Write them down and set aside dedicated time to worry about them later.

BREATHE INTO YOUR BELLY
Anxiety triggers muscle tension across the body. Consciously relax your abdominal muscles by taking slow deep breaths into your belly, in through the nose and out through the mouth.

MAKE A SELF-SOOTHE BOX
Prepare for anxious moments by filling a small box with comforting objects. Add one item for each sense to soothe the brain's fear centre.

TAKE A BATH
A hot afternoon bath can change your mood. The warm water relaxes your muscles, resets your body clock, and improves your sleep.

TALK TO SOMEONE
Sharing anxious thoughts with someone else can help to break the cycle of rumination. Speak to a trusted friend, a mental health professional or a helpline listener.

WALK IT OFF
Fight or flight chemistry prepares the body to get up and go, so exercise is a good way to put the body's overreaction to good use.

TRACK DOWN YOUR TRIGGERS
It can be hard to work out what triggers anxiety. Keep a journal to help spot those hidden patterns and learn to work around them.

ASK FOR HELP
Don't wait for your anxiety to get really bad before you ask for professional help. It can be easier to manage if you seek help early.

If you, or anyone you know, is affected by anxiety, the following charities and helplines are ready to offer free support.

UK
Mind www.mind.org.uk
Samaritans 116 123

US
Anxiety and Depression Association of America https://adaa.org/
National Alliance on Mental Illness (NAMI) 1-800-950-NAMI (6264)

Australia
SANE Australia www.sane.org
Lifeline 13 11 14

type of anxiety disorder. Sometimes one disorder directly causes another. Other times, several disorders have the same underlying causes, making people likely to develop them in combination.

Treatments
The frontline treatment for those struggling is cognitive behavioural therapy (CBT), a talking therapy that helps people learn to break out of cycles of negative thoughts. It encourages people to look closely at the connections between their thoughts, feelings, physical sensations and actions.

According to researchers at the Norwegian University of Science and Technology, CBT is far more effective than medication for treating anxiety. Drug treatments might dampen the physical and psychological symptoms, but the effects are often only temporary. CBT addresses negative thought patterns directly. In a trial that compared the two types of treatment, 85% of participants improved using CBT alone.

One of the challenges in treating anxiety is the amount of time it takes for people to come forward and ask for help. According to a paper published in *Nature Reviews*, it often takes between three and 30 years. But research has also shown that asking for help early can make anxiety easier to manage.

DO ANIMALS GET ANXIOUS?

The brain chemistry that triggers anxiety evolved because it is essential for our survival. The pathways that drive our overactive fear response are the same ones that underpin our ability to sense and respond to real threats. We share those pathways with all other mammals, making it likely that they are capable of experiencing anxiety too. It's hard for scientists to measure anxiety in animals because they can't tell us how they're feeling. But their behaviour can be a giveaway. In dogs, for example, separation from a trusted owner can trigger the same kinds of physical anxiety symptoms seen in humans. They become agitated, their muscles tremble, and they can be sick or lose control of their bowels. Treatment for anxiety in animals is similar, too. It involves making them feel safe, providing distractions during distressing situations, and seeking professional support when it becomes too much to manage at home.

UNDERSTANDING OVERWHELM

Understanding
OVERWHELM

More of us than ever are struggling with feeling overwhelmed in our everyday lives, but what does this mean and how can we prevent it?

WORDS JULIE BASSETT

Overwhelm can creep up on you. Your to-do list just keeps building, the emails are flying into your inbox, the calendar is packed with appointments and reminders, deadlines are looming closer... Your stress levels rise until one day it hits you, and you feel totally overwhelmed and unable to comprehend how you're supposed to do everything you need to do.

Overwhelm, by definition, means that there's 'too much to deal with'; and just like a boat overwhelmed with water, unable to stay afloat, everything you have on your plate can drag you down, leaving you feeling panicked, anxious and unable to see a way forward.

Why are we so overwhelmed?
We all get to the point where we feel like it's just impossible to get everything done, but this doesn't always lead to overwhelm. That feeling of being completely unable to cope with anything else can be scary and worrying, and it can seem like you're the only one feeling like this. But statistics show that feeling overwhelmed is far from a rare experience. A survey conducted by the Mental Health Foundation in 2018 found that 74% of adults in the UK felt so stressed that they were overwhelmed or unable to cope. Similarly, data from the American Psychological Association in its Stress in America 2022 report, showed 27% reporting that most days they are so stressed they cannot function.

Overwhelm can come from lots of different places. For many, it can be down to work responsibilities, an excessive workload, or working in a particularly stressful environment. Some job types are especially prone to overwhelm due to the nature of the role. For example, one report[1] showed that more than two thirds of health and social care workers in the UK were feeling overwhelmed due to longer hours and increased pressures in the time since the Covid-19 pandemic. However, any of us can feel overwhelmed at work, especially when juggling it around family responsibilities.

Other causes of overwhelm can be closer to home, including things like worrying about family members, grief after the loss of a loved one, financial worries, relationship problems, health concerns and so on. Any of these things are incredibly stressful in themselves, but when they happen at a time when you already have a lot on, then it can be even more difficult to cope. For some, the overwhelm comes from external factors. Changing environmental factors, for example, or political issues, can create a general feeling of being out of control, which can exacerbate overwhelm.

Overwhelm can come about as a result of one big change in your life, or it can be the build up of lots of stress factors piling up on top of each other. It can also be more likely during a period of poor mental health, when it can be harder to cope with everything happening at once.

Some of us are more prone to overwhelm than others. We all cope with stress differently and have different responses to stressful situations. What might lead to overwhelm in one person, would be a minor stress factor for another. Overwhelm is more likely for those with an existing mental health condition, such as depression or anxiety, or for those already under a lot of stress. If you struggle with regulating your emotions, you may also be more likely to suffer from overwhelm, and this can mean that those with ADHD or autism can also feel overwhelmed more often. According to a Mental Health Foundation study, more women than men experience overwhelm. It can also be more common for those who have a tendency towards perfectionism and high achievers.

Signs of overwhelm
Overwhelm goes beyond feelings of »

> " OVERWHELM IS MORE LIKELY FOR THOSE WITH AN EXISTING MENTAL HEALTH CONDITION "

MANAGE YOUR MIND

UNDERSTANDING OVERWHELM

UNDERSTANDING OVERWHELM

INSTANT RELIEF FROM OVERWHELM

When you feel overwhelm creeping in, there are some quick strategies to help calm you down

TAKE A BREAK
If you're trying to push through a task but feel completely overwhelmed, then stop. You're not helping by forcing yourself to keep going, and the more you try, the more your brain will resist. Step away from what you're doing and find a quiet space for a few minutes. This can help you to refocus and reset.

BREATHING EXERCISE
Slow your breath down and start to focus on it. Breathe deeply in and out, five counts in, five counts out. Try to switch off all your other thoughts and only notice your breathing. This can help to regulate your emotions.

START AGAIN
Write down what's bothering you and prioritise. Think about what you have to do right this moment, and what can wait a little bit or be delegated to someone else. This can help you refocus and put your energy into the right tasks.

---

normal, everyday stress. When you're feeling overwhelmed, you might experience both physical and mental symptoms.

Most people notice the mental side of overwhelm initially. First it can manifest as an inability to focus or concentrate, and you may find that you're procrastinating more, unable to get started on a task. Your brain can feel like it's frozen, leaving you unable to move forward or complete even the simplest of tasks. You may find it hard to think rationally, blowing things out of proportion or overreacting to situations that wouldn't normally faze you. With all of this, you may then find it hard to prioritise what you need to do, leaving you stressed about getting everything done while also feeling utterly incapable of doing anything at all. And while your brain is running on high alert like this, you will likely find it difficult to make decisions or solve problems.

Once this level of overwhelm takes over, you might find that you start to withdraw from people, including friends and family, as well as at work. This could be due to embarrassment that you're struggling to keep on top of things, or a feeling that they won't understand how you're feeling. Without external support, you'll likely mull everything over in your mind, making you feel anxious, stressed and low. This can impact on your mood, leaving you irritable, angry and hopeless. You may find that you cry more easily or snap when someone asks you a question.

Alongside these mental symptoms, some will find that they also feel the stress and overwhelm in their body too. Many people report headaches, stomach problems, a tight chest, headaches, fatigue, insomnia, aches and pains, and a faster heartbeat.

No matter how much you try to apply logic and rational thought to your situation, your body has gone into a state of high stress and anxiety. Daily life can start to feel very hard. While the original overwhelm may have been triggered by bigger traumas or stressors, by the point that it takes over, even small decisions like deciding what to wear or what to have for dinner can feel too much. This can lead to a complete shutdown, where you can't cope with normal day-to-day life and you retreat into yourself. Some people find that they end up staying at home more, or spending more time in bed, as everything else feels too hard. And you likely know that this isn't helping, but feel too mentally drained and exhausted to make the necessary changes to lift you out of the situation.

However, if you're suffering from overwhelm and you leave it unchecked, it can lead to more serious mental health conditions, such as severe anxiety or depression. The first step is recognising that

MANAGE YOUR MIND

UNDERSTANDING OVERWHELM

what you're experiencing is overwhelm, then you can start to take small steps to help overcome it and, going forward, prevent it from happening again.

Reducing overwhelm
It can be really hard to break out of the overwhelm cycle once you're in it. Life doesn't stop and it can feel like your to-do list is building up around you. You can't cope with what's happening, so you freeze and don't get tasks done, which then means you get behind and end up with even more to do, which leads to more overwhelm. So, the key is breaking that cycle and reinstating a sense of perspective.

When we're in a state of overwhelm, we can lose ability to apply logic. Worry, panic and fear can take over, and we start thinking irrationally and catastrophising our situation. Sometimes it can be helpful to express these feelings somewhere, which can be by talking them through with a trusted friend or family member, or writing them down in a journal. Often, just by going through the process of explaining how you're feeling can help you to see things in a more rational way.

It can help to write down everything that you're feeling overwhelmed by, no matter how small it might be. By seeing it all in one place, you may be able to get some fresh perspective. It might be that it doesn't look as big when it's written down. Or you might see that what you have on your plate is far too much and that you need some help to tackle your stressors. Once you have everything that's worrying you written down, start to categorise your thoughts in a non-judgemental and compassionate way. There will likely be a mix of stressors that are in your control and those that are outside of it. For those things that you can control, identify tasks you need to do to reduce that stress. Try to separate out urgent tasks that have to be done – your non-negotiables – then split this into things that have to be tackled by you personally and things you can delegate. Everything else can be sorted by priority, to help you see that not everything has to be done right now. Anything that is out of your control needs to be acknowledged – it is contributing to your overwhelm – but with a gentle reminder to yourself there are some situations you can't influence.

When you're in this state of overwhelm, the priority for your wellbeing is bringing it back under control, and making a plan to help you feel calmer and more on top of things. Once you are in a stronger place and feel less overwhelmed, then you need to put in place healthy practices to help prevent it in the future. Make sure that you have time every week to do things that bring you joy, whether that's a hobby, self-care or reading a favourite book, for example. Also make sure that you're moving your body and spending time in nature. Get into good habits with task management, ensuring that you assign a priority to what needs to be done when, and delegating when you can. Keeping a daily journal can help a great deal – many people find that a morning diary can help with setting intentions for the day, which can build focus and help prevent things from building up.

Above all, treat yourself with compassion and kindness. When everything piles up around you, it can be hard to let go of what you can't control and prioritise what you can, but it gets easier with practice.

LEARNING TO DO LESS

Part of the reason we get overwhelmed is that we're simply trying to achieve too much. We want to perform well at work, look after our families, exercise regularly, cook healthy meals, keep the house clean, see our friends and so on. The problem is we end up with to-do lists that are impossible to finish. 'Less is more' has never been truer. Try to identify areas where you could do less. For example, you don't have to say yes to every social invite – pick events that make you feel joy, rather than those you feel obliged to attend. Make extra portions of meals to stick in the freezer so you can have some easy nights when you don't need to cook, or plan some simple meals with very little prep. Don't fill every evening with activities and have some time when you can relax. You're in control of what you fill your life with, so make time for what's important and embrace doing less of the things that are not.

WHAT IS BRAIN FOG?

WHAT IS
Brain Fog?

Feeling fuzzy, struggling to concentrate, and finding it hard to remember things? This could be brain fog, but what is this and why does it happen?

WHAT IS BRAIN FOG?

WORDS JULIE BASSETT

You might have come across the term 'brain fog' before, a phrase that's used to describe a state in which you feel mentally tired, are unable to focus or concentrate on tasks, have poor memory, and just feel sluggish, like your brain isn't firing like it should.

Chances are that we've all experienced brain fog at some point. If you're having trouble sleeping, for example, this can lead to feeling slow and fuzzy. Ongoing and chronic brain fog can be hard to cope with, particularly in situations where you need to be fully alert, such as at work, driving or caring for children. Brain fog can manifest in lots of different ways, from becoming forgetful over appointments to finding it hard to recall information. It can be frustrating, especially if you're usually mentally sharp, and it can lead to you feeling overwhelmed by everyday tasks, particularly if they seem to be taking much longer than normal to complete.

Causes of brain fog

Brain fog is an informal term, and isn't a diagnosis or condition. It's not, for example, like dementia, as it doesn't change the structure of your brain. It's usually a symptom, so the key lies in discovering and treating the root cause. Brain fog can be caused by certain medical conditions, both physical and mental. Mental health conditions like depression, anxiety and chronic stress can be draining and lead to cognitive disruption. When you're overly stressed, your body switches into a survival state, shutting down any surplus processes, reducing our capacity to engage in everyday tasks. Anxiety can lead to difficulties in concentrating or confusion.

Brain fog can also result from illness, particularly after a virus. Covid-19 is associated with cases of brain fog, particularly in those with long Covid (see the box top-right). Some forms of brain fog are so common among certain diseases that they have coined their own terms. 'Fibro fog', for example, refers to those who suffer from cognitive dysfunction related to fibromyalgia or chronic fatigue syndrome. Similarly, 'chemo brain' is a type of brain fog that is commonly experienced by those who undergo certain cancer treatments. Some medications can cause brain fog too, including antihistamines, antidepressants, painkillers and sleep aids. And then there are hormone-related periods of brain fog, which are experienced by some women when they are pregnant or going through menopause.

Beating brain fog

Treating brain fog depends on the ultimate cause of it. If brain fog is being triggered by a medication, for example, then simply switching to a different type can be enough to solve the problem. If it's being caused by a specific external stressor, such as a bad night's sleep, jet lag or worrying about something, then it usually passes once that stressor is resolved. If brain fog is persistent and doesn't seem to lift, then it may require medical intervention to help find and treat the root cause.

But there are some lifestyle interventions that seem to work well for all kinds of brain fog. Sleep is a key factor – the more sleep you lose, the worse your brain fog. Making sleep a priority, therefore, can have a significant impact on your brain function, no matter what the underlying cause. Things like making sure your bedroom is dark enough, getting into bed at the same time every day, keeping your room cool, and not looking at your phone too close to bedtime can all help.

Another key factor is exercise. It's one of the most commonly recommended treatments, giving your brain function a boost but also helping to support your sleep. If your brain fog is caused by a condition that makes it hard to exercise, even a little can help. Short walks and fresh air can have a huge impact. It's about little and often, rather than hardcore gym sessions and running marathons. There is also some evidence that your diet can play a part in combatting brain fog too, prioritising those foods that reduce inflammation (such as ginger, leafy greens, berries and turmeric), as well as foods that help boost brain health (oily fish, nuts and seeds, fruits and vegetables).

Limiting stress, practising mindfulness, keeping a journal, and drinking plenty of water can all help symptoms too, as can cognitive behavioural therapy (CBT) in long-term cases, helping you to manage your symptoms and reframe your thoughts around them.

For those who suffer from chronic brain fog it can be a frustrating experience, especially as it's not an obvious condition to those on the outside and it's hard to explain. A trip to the doctor is usually a good first step, as it can help to recognise the problem and start to put strategies into place.

BRAIN FOG AND COVID

While brain fog has always been around, there has been a lot of research done regarding its link to Covid. Brain fog has been extensively reported and experienced by those who have had the infection, particularly in people who have long Covid (where symptoms have persisted beyond 12 weeks). One study[1], published in early 2024, found that those with long Covid have measurable memory and cognitive impact, and even those who recovered more quickly may experience brain fog for a year or more after the infection. In fact, the analysis showed an equivalent of three IQ points difference in test scores between those who had had an infection and those who hadn't, and an equivalent of six IQ points for those with unresolved symptoms that persisted for more than 12 weeks. While experts still don't know why brain fog exists as a symptom, large-scale research studies like this do show that it is a common side effect and worthy of further investigation.

> "IT CAN BE FRUSTRATING, ESPECIALLY IF YOU'RE USUALLY MENTALLY SHARP"

[1] Cognition and Memory after Covid-19 in a Large Community Sample, Hampshire, Adam et al, N Engl J Med, 2024.

BUILDING TO A BURNOUT

BUILDING TO A *Burnout*

Burnout is on the rise, with more of us experiencing it than ever, but what is fuelling this increase and what can you do about it?

WORDS JULIE BASSETT

Are you feeling tired, exhausted or drained most of the time? Maybe a bit overwhelmed, procrastinating on tasks, or taking longer to do them? Feeling detached, alone, negative or helpless? Do you feel like life is getting on top of you and you're unable to keep up with the demands of your to-do list at work or at home? These are all signs that you could be heading towards a burnout, a state of physical or mental exhaustion that is usually triggered by long-term exposure to stressors.

In today's modern world, the pressure is on to do everything and do everything well. It's all around us, within our own social circles but also through social media, where we can see a glimpse of what other people's lives look like (what they choose to show us anyway). Burnout is on the rise globally – and it's no wonder. We're in a perfect storm, where on one hand we're pushing ourselves harder than ever to achieve at work and at home, while also being made to feel like taking any rest is 'lazy' or 'unproductive' by outside influences.

Bex Spiller, founder of The Anti-Burnout Club (theantiburnoutclub.com), explains: "When we've been going at full speed for so long, trying to keep all of the plates spinning at once, it feels strange when you suddenly slam on the brakes. The thing is, this perception that self-care is selfish or unproductive has often come from somewhere else, so one of the best ways to start reframing this is to work out who or where this perception comes from in the first place." Bex suggests that this perception might come from friends or family members making you feel like you're being selfish for taking any time to yourself, or a toxic boss who guilt trips you for taking time off. "For me, learned behaviour from my parents and 'hustle hard' influencers made me feel as though rest was for the weak... But once I realised this perception was part of their beliefs »

> ❝ IN TODAY'S MODERN WORLD, THE PRESSURE IS ON TO DO EVERYTHING AND DO EVERYTHING WELL ❞

EXPERT BURNOUT TIPS

BEX SPILLER
FOUNDER OF THE ANTI-BURNOUT CLUB

Bex Spiller is a multi-award-winning expert in burnout, stress and overwhelm, author, TEDx speaker, and founder of the free mental health and wellbeing app, The Anti-Burnout Club.

THEANTIBURNOUTCLUB.COM

What would you say to someone who was experiencing burnout right now?

Becoming burnt out didn't happen overnight, so please don't try to rush your recovery! It took me several attempts to recover from burnout before I realised I was falling into what I now call the Cycle of (Un)Wellness. This is where you:

- *start feeling stressed and overwhelmed as there's just too much to do*
- promise yourself you'll look after yourself when there's less to do
- *feel burnt out and have to take time off*
- cram in some wellbeing until you can get back to that to-do list
- *come back to an even bigger to-do list than before*
- start feeling stressed and overwhelmed as there's just too much to do

And so the cycle continues! Recovery doesn't mean just taking some time off and then falling straight back into old patterns. Yes, you will likely need some time off (and most health professionals will advise you of this). But what's important is what you do when life returns to normal. How can you fit little pockets of self-care into your daily life to help you find more balance?

What three daily habits do you think are the most important when it comes to preventing burnout?

FOCUS ON THE BASICS FIRST

We get so swept up in new wellbeing trends that we often neglect the essentials: getting enough sleep, drinking enough water, and eating food that makes us feel good. Get the basics in order and everything else will start to fall into place.

BRAIN DUMP

Our brains aren't designed to retain all the information we feel we have to nowadays, so regular brain dumping is a must. At the end of your day, dump everything out of your head and onto paper to help reduce stress and overwhelm.

CHECK IN WITH YOURSELF

Throughout the day, have regular check-ins with yourself to start noticing if stress levels are creeping up. You can do this in your head, in an app or in a journal. Connecting with yourself is vital for recognising any warning signs before it's too late. It could just be, 'How am I really feeling right now?' or a whole page of journal prompts – what matters is it fits into your life and becomes a habit.

---

and values, not mine, it made it much easier to give myself permission to rest."

Burnout doesn't look the same for everyone. Common symptoms include struggling to sleep or sleeping too much, feeling fatigued, finding it hard to do normal daily tasks, feeling emotionally drained, a sense of apathy and detachment, and a feeling of dread or anxiety. This can impact on your mental health, as you struggle to regain a sense of balance. You may also find that when you're feeling burned out, other areas of your life start to suffer; it's not uncommon to drink more than usual, eat less well and neglect exercise – all things we know are connected to poorer mental health.

Risk factors for burnout

Burnout is something that anyone can experience. You don't have to be a corporate executive to feel the pressure at work, and you don't have to have a house full of children to burn out at home. "From what I've seen in the three years running The Anti-Burnout Club, burnout can impact anyone at any time; the only common denominator is some kind of chronic stressor," says Bex. "While the WHO defines it as an 'occupational phenomenon', I've seen people burnt out from work, home life, chronic conditions, and caregiving. If there's something that's making you feel chronically stressed, it can lead to burnout."

Some of us are more at risk than others. For example, if you are a perfectionist, setting constantly high standards and wanting to always achieve the best you possibly can, then you may feel chronically stressed more easily and more frequently. Extensive research conducted by Professor Gordon Parker, outlined in his 2022 book *A Guide to Identifying Burnout and Pathways to Recovery*, found that people who are perfectionists are more likely to head towards burnout as a result of their own 'unrelenting standards'.

Those who are prone to 'people please' may also be more likely to experience burnout, as they put the needs of others over and above their own, neglecting their wellbeing until it reaches a point of burnout. Similarly, those who are high achievers, particularly in the workplace, may also neglect self-care, work longer hours and pile on enormous amounts of pressure to meet their goals. One study by Asana[1], a project management tool, also identified a crossover between those who suffer from imposter syndrome and burnout.

Burnout in the workplace

While burnout can impact anyone, work-life balance is still one of the biggest contributors to burnout. Workplace culture

BUILDING TO A BURNOUT

can increasingly lead to burnout, thanks to unrealistic targets, increasing workload, longer hours, higher expectations, a sense of always being available, a blurring of lines between home and work life, and so on. It's no wonder, then, that there are so many studies conducted in the workplace that show a significant number of people experiencing burnout. Future Forum Pulse (futureforum.com) is a quarterly survey of more than 10,000 workers from around the world. Its winter 2023 report showed that burnout is reported by 43% of the workforce. The same survey also showed that more women than men reported experiencing burnout (46% to 37%), and age is a factor too – those under 30 reported more incidence of burnout than those above 30.

While there are things we can do personally to try to rebalance our work and home lives, some responsibility has to lie with employers themselves. Addressing a toxic or stressful workplace can help to give employees a chance to maintain their wellbeing, while also achieving at work. And this has to be more than signposting online resources, doing a one-off workshop or sending an email. "Employers should be helping employees create space and balance by encouraging and respecting boundaries," says Bex. "Ensuring workload is realistic, promoting workplace wellbeing initiatives throughout the organisation, and giving people the time to actually enjoy them too! Creating an open and honest workplace where employees feel comfortable talking about how they feel and can also spot the warning signs are two huge steps towards reducing burnout at work."

The Future Forum Pulse survey found that flexibility was a key factor in whether a person was more at risk of burnout – those unsatisfied with the level of flexibility in their work life were 43% more likely to say that they feel burned out at work than those who are happy with their level of flexibility. Of course, working from home, either fully or hybrid, brings with it its own problems. It can be harder to make that separation, and also when it comes to knowing when to switch off – it's so easy to jump on and answer a query when you're metres away from your computer at all times.

Some simple, practical measures can help, advises Bex: "I'd always recommend separating your physical work and home space as much as possible. Even if you don't have a separate office space, being able to pack up or hide any work equipment and materials is vital. If you can see work-related stuff, chances are you'll be constantly reminding yourself of your to-do list. The same goes for being able to turn off work-related notifications on your devices too. If you don't have separate work phones, then most phones will let you change your settings to only get certain notifications at certain times."

How to take action

If you feel like you're heading towards burnout, or already there, it's important to first recognise that. Admitting that you're burned out and need to rest – properly rest – can be difficult, especially if you feel like you can't just stop doing everything on your to-do list, whether that's at work or at home.

One thing that can help is to regain a sense of perspective. If you're struggling with being able to step away from work, for example, Bex recommends this activity, something that she does herself if she finds that she's slipping back into old patterns: "Ask yourself: 'What do I want to be remembered for when I'm gone? Do I want someone to stand up at my funeral and say, 'Well, she worked SO hard we never really saw her', or do I want them to tell stories about the amazing times they had with me when I wasn't working? I know it often sounds a little morbid to think about, but it's an ideal pattern interrupt that will stop you in your tracks when you go to open that email on a weekend."

Next, make sure you plan in some time for you – but don't overplan either. Sometimes what you need is a complete stop to reset – a day or two with no expectations and demands. Watch that boxset, catch up on sleep, read a book, go for a gentle walk. Then, once you start to feel a little better, take some time to think about what you need to do to make your daily life more sustainable. Do you need help in any particular area? Are there changes you can make to bring back a better sense of balance?

Talking to friends and family can be a useful exercise – they might not be aware of how pressured and stressed out you're feeling. If you feel you can, it's also worth having a conversation at work, if that's something that's contributing to your burnout. You may want to talk to a professional if you're struggling to identify the changes you need to make, or if you feel you need someone more removed from the situation to give you a different perspective.

The most important thing, however, is not to ignore the way you're feeling. Burnout is very real, and won't get better without some kind of intervention, self-care and rest. If you ignore it, it can get worse, causing real damage to your physical and mental health, leaving you unable to meet the demands of your job or home life. It's much better to learn to recognise your signs, and take action before it's too late. ■

> " PEOPLE PLEASERS AND PERFECTIONISTS ARE MORE AT RISK "

MANAGE YOUR MIND

37

¹ Asana's Anatomy of Work Special Report

HOW TO *STRESS* Better

You can't escape it entirely, but stress isn't all bad, and there are ways to harness it to your advantage

WORDS JENNY ROWE

According to a 2024 survey by Ciphr, 86% of UK adults feel stressed at least once a month, and 11% experience stress every day, with tiredness, money and loved ones being the leading causes. But we shouldn't be scared of stress. "It's normal," says psychotherapist Caron Barruw, co-founder of The Niche Group. "It's how we manage it that makes the difference."

We can learn to turn stress into something more useful – helpful even, adds neuroscientist and author of *Psycho-Logical*, Dr Dean Burnett. Sound good? Here's how to harness and not hate all stress.

A helping hand

"Stress is the brain's threat detection system preparing us to deal with danger," says Dr Burnett. It mostly feels unpleasant, but on a fundamental level it keeps us safe. "While it is usually the consequence of a negative situation, there may be positive outcomes," says Caron. This is more likely if we are working towards a goal that we believe is positive too, such as interviewing for a new job, getting married or running a race.

Ultimately, an optimal dose of stress can help us perform better. "The stress response increases muscle tension and raises heart and breathing rate, which makes you more focused, less distractible and more motivated," says Dr Burnett. Whatever you're feeling stressed about, this physiological reaction means you are more likely to complete the task to the best of your ability. This is stress in its positive form, which is known as eustress.

Striking a balance

"Countless studies have shown that, up to a point, a person's performance increases directly in proportion to how much stress they're experiencing," says Dr Burnett. However, if stress levels continue past this point, we start to struggle. "This increases our stress levels again and we can get stuck in a stress cycle," says Caron.

The main issue with stress is when you have too much of it for too long – this is when acute stress morphs into chronic, more harmful stress. "When stress is constant, it's like keeping your foot on the accelerator," says Caron. "It leads to burnout."

Breaking point

Stress is sneaky. It can be easy to keep cruising through life, not realising you're approaching burnout – until you're there. "Our brains aren't particularly good at noticing changes that happen over long periods," says Dr Burnett. "But it can be done, particularly if the changes caused by stress are marked."

You may be struggling to sleep, have low or high appetite, headaches, low sexual desire or high blood pressure. If you are unable to finish tasks, feel tearful, worry all the time or snap at people when you normally wouldn't, then stress may be affecting your wellbeing and it's time to get help.

It's important to recognise that there is a difference between coping with stress and dealing with it. "Dealing with stress involves processing stressful emotions and actively bringing about changes that address the cause of stress," says Dr Burnett. "Coping is just putting up with the stressful situation and carrying on, which is not a great long-term strategy, as our capacity for tolerating stress will max out eventually."

How to stress better

So can we become better at dealing with stress and stop it tipping us over the edge? In short, yes. Like musicians, dancers and actors who are taught to reinterpret their nerves as excitement, it's possible to change our emotional reactions to stressful experiences into something more positive – though obviously this depends on the situation, and mainly applies to small-scale day-to-day dramas.

Optimists who choose to see potential daily stressors (such as traffic jams and chores) as challenges rather than threats before emotions flare up, reduce the negative impact of stress, as shown in a recent two-decade-long study[1].

You can also try to increase your threshold for stress. "By taking on new challenges and pushing yourself beyond your comfort zone – but in ways that you feel OK with – you could gradually increase the amount of stress you're capable of dealing with," says Dr Burnett.

KNOW YOUR STRESSORS

To stress better (and less), we need to know our triggers. Stress trackers monitor things like heart rate variability (the variation in time between each heart beat) to measure stress levels and help us identify our personal triggers – so we can come up with solutions. The key to successful stress tracking is to ensure you're asking, 'Why am I stressed?', not the less useful question, 'How stressed am I?', says Dr Burnett.

TRY IT Most fitness wearables now have stress tracking capabilities, or you can try the StressScan app for free (Apple, Google Play). At its simplest, stress tracking could just mean keeping a stress diary. "Rate the stress from 1-10 as it happens," says Caron. "This will help you feel in control of the stress rather than the stress controlling you."

"WE CAN LEARN TO TURN STRESS INTO SOMETHING MORE USEFUL"

[1] The Journals of Gerontology

PANICKED? PRESS PAUSE

40

MANAGE YOUR MIND

PANICKED? Press Pause

It's easier than you think to take back control when you're having a panic attack

WORDS ROSE GOODMAN

A pounding heart, crushing chest pain and debilitating terror may sound like the signs of a heart attack, but for those who suffer from panic attacks, these scary symptoms are all too common. Sound familiar? You're not alone – up to a third of people will experience at least one panic attack in their lifetime[1], while others will have regular attacks or several in a short space of time.

Whatever your experience, there are ways to bring a panic attack under control. Here, our experts explain what could help...

What happens?
"A panic attack is an intense emotional and physical response to a sense of dread or fear," says psychologist Dr Alison McClymont. "It may have an obvious trigger (such as being under stress), but it may also come on seemingly unprovoked and can make you feel as if your health – or, in extreme situations, your life – is under threat."

Spot the signs
The overwhelming symptom of a panic attack is a sense of impending doom or anxiety. "This may be accompanied by difficulty breathing (hyperventilating), sweaty palms, a racing heart or muscle pain," explains Dr McClymont. Trembling, dizziness and feeling detached from reality are also common symptoms.

The physical symptoms can be so extreme that some sufferers may go to A&E, believing they are having a heart »

SUPPORTING A LOVED ONE

If you're with someone who is experiencing a panic attack, it can be difficult to know how to help. But there are some simple ways you can help make them feel safe and at ease. "Don't touch them. Speak calmly and slowly, remind them where they are, that they are safe, and that you are there," says Dr McClymont. "Try modelling slow, calm breathing (in for four and out for eight), get them some water and keep reminding them that this will pass, and that breathing is the key."

5 WAYS TO PREVENT AN ATTACK

These daily habits can help to reduce future panic attacks, says the Mental Health Foundation:

1. Practise better breathing (do the 4-7-8 breathing technique daily).

2. *Take regular exercise, such as walking or yoga. This will help to reduce stress and improve your mood.*

3. Eat frequent meals to stabilise blood-sugar levels.

4. *Avoid caffeine, alcohol and smoking.*

5. Try mindfulness to bring you back to the present moment. Download the Calm app (*£7.99/$14.99 per month, iOS and Android*).

---

attack. However, while panic attacks are frightening, they're not dangerous and won't cause you physical harm.

Stay calm
If you feel a panic attack developing, try to think of it like a big wave. You cannot stop it, but you can ride it. "Distract yourself from catastrophic thoughts and don't buy into them," says Dr Paul McLaren, consultant psychiatrist for the Priory Group. There are also things you can do to take back a feeling of control.

JUST BREATHE
"Try to slow your breathing, even though you will feel that you need to breathe harder," says Dr McLaren. This 4-7-8 breathing exercise will help activate your parasympathetic nervous system, which is responsible for relaxation.

1. Close your mouth and inhale through your nose for a count of four.

2. Now hold your breath for a count of seven.

3. Exhale completely out of your mouth, making a 'whoosh' sound, for a count of eight.

4. Inhale again and repeat the cycle three more times, or more if needed.

GROUND YOURSELF
Try the 5,4,3,2,1 grounding technique, which will bring you back to the present moment. This exercise requires you to engage all of your senses by naming:

Five things you can see.

Four things you feel, such as the texture of a chair or the temperature of the room you're in.

Three things you can hear.

Two things you can smell.

One thing you can taste. If you can't taste anything, name a taste you like.

NOTICE YOUR BODY
A body-scan exercise can release tension you're not even aware you're holding. Practising this technique regularly can help reduce anxiety, depression and fatigue. During a panic attack, doing this exercise can help to bring you back to your body and feel safe within it. Give it a go:

Sit or lie down in a comfortable spot and position.

Start with the breathing strategy described in the previous column and then focus on your toes.

Check in with what you can feel and how they feel. Give them a little wiggle.

Move on to the soles of your feet. Keep breathing slowly and gradually move up through your body, checking in, moving and relaxing each part as you go.

When you've completed this, gradually go back down your body in the same order whilst continuing your slow and steady breath style. This can be a really useful activity to help you de-stress and be more mindful and body aware.

IMAGINE A SAFE SPACE
Also known as visualisation, this technique requires you to imagine that you're in a calm, safe and soothing place. "Think about what you can see, hear, taste, smell and feel," says clinical psychologist Dr Marianne Trent, creator of The Feel Better Academy. "Know that you can revisit this place in your mind whenever you choose." Your safe space could be anywhere – from a tropical beach or your garden in the summer, to a relaxing bubble bath.

BE AWARE
Feeling stressed out? Integrative counsellor Katharina Wolf suggests using a technique called AWARE, which works to move your brain from a state of high anxiety to a place of calm, and helps to avoid creating further triggers.

Accept the anxiety/panic. Fighting it will only heighten it.

Watch and scale your panic/anxiety from one to ten (with ten being maximum panic/anxiety).

Act normally, while imagining yourself calm.

Repeat the above three steps.

Expect the best. Use positive statements such as, 'This can't harm me'; 'I can master this'; 'This will go away soon'.

Rest and recover
It's common to feel exhausted and emotional after suffering a panic attack. "Go to a calm and quiet place. Play some music and take time to comfort yourself and re-engage with your surroundings," advises Dr McClymont. "Drink water and, if you feel dizzy, try eating a small amount of sugar. The most important thing is to be still, breathe, and show yourself

compassion for the intense and frightening experience you have just endured."

Panic attack or anxiety attack?
While these terms are often used interchangeably, the symptoms of a panic attack and an anxiety attack do differ slightly. "An anxiety attack is usually not accompanied by such a sense of impending doom or death," says Dr McClymont. "The physical symptoms are similar, but in a panic attack the threat response is more highly elevated and things such as hyperventilating or chest pain are more likely to occur."

Stop the cycle
Talking therapies such as cognitive behavioural therapy (CBT) are often used to treat panic attacks. "It is likely that panic developed for an important reason to protect you from something painful or difficult, says Dr Trent. "Working through these reasons and learning more about why you respond in the way you do can be incredibly useful, and enable you to enjoy your life more fully."

> **IT'S COMMON TO FEEL EXHAUSTED AND EMOTIONAL AFTER SUFFERING A PANIC ATTACK**

Is it panic disorder?
If you experience panic attacks, it doesn't necessarily mean that you have panic disorder. As Dr McClymont explains, panic disorder is classified as having at least one panic attack and subsequent fear or intrusive thoughts about having another, across one month.

If you're resorting to unhealthy coping mechanisms or ways of preventing an attack – for example, avoiding certain situations that have caused you anxiety in the past – you may be diagnosed with panic disorder. However, this can only be diagnosed by a professional and may require both medication and therapy to treat it, so visit your doctor if you are concerned.

'I BEAT THE FEAR'

Dr Sophie Mort, clinical psychologist and the author of *A Manual For Being Human*[2] (£14.99/$18.50, Simon & Schuster), shares her experience of overcoming panic attacks...

"I had my first panic attack aged 18, when I was on holiday. I kept telling myself I had sunstroke, which was why I overheated and my heart was racing. Then the next day it came back, over and over. I knew then that it wasn't the sun.

My panic attacks then escalated to the point where I didn't leave the house for nearly three months, as everything I did set them off. I quit university and didn't see friends.

I finally saw a therapist and she taught me techniques to manage the panic. After a month, I noticed that the attacks had lessened enough for me to leave the house. I haven't had a panic attack in years, and I manage my anxiety with yoga, mindfulness and breathing exercises.

My favourite technique is saying 'bring it on' whenever I feel the physical sensations of anxiety or panic building. That's been the most important part of my journey, because when I say it and really mean it, it removes the fear cycle that kept the panic alive."

Coping WITH PTSD

How can a single traumatic event cause day-to-day distress?

WORDS AILSA HARVEY

After experiencing a scary, painful or harrowing event, you would hope to feel some form of relief when it is over. For one in three people who experience trauma, however, the aftermath of such a time is long-term mental scarring, in the form of post-traumatic stress disorder (PTSD).

Suffering from PTSD involves being forced to relive some of the worst and most traumatic days of your life. Whether being terrorised during sleep by vivid nightmares, or experiencing flashbacks during the day, PTSD can leave people feeling like they have no escape and are unable to move on from the past. This is when the brain puts up its defence to protect itself, but ends up with an overactive alarm system. Your alarm system is always functioning, working to alert you when danger is detected, but when too stimulated it can physically drain the rest of the body.

PTSD can be caused by a range of events, but always includes a factor of feeling severely unsafe or at risk of dying. Traumatic incidents don't necessarily need to be directly experienced by you for you to be impacted long term. All it takes is to witness or hear second-hand about a severely traumatic event to trigger PTSD. Not everyone who experiences a traumatic event will develop it, and it has proven most common in people who have existing anxiety or depression. Not only that, but doctors think those who have a parent with a mental health disorder are also more at risk.

What are the symptoms?

As a disorder that is defined by mental and emotional distress, the possible symptoms are relatively broad. The most commonly associated symptoms involve reliving a traumatic event through mostly uncontrollable flashbacks and nightmares.

The difference between a memory and a flashback is that while you recall a memory, you remain aware that the event is in the past. Contrastingly, flashbacks fool you into thinking that the event is happening right now.

Flashbacks aren't the same for all people. Some sufferers describe their flashbacks as if they are watching the series of events as a detailed and unwanted video. Others only visualise partial images of what happened and some people's flashbacks contain no visuals at all. Smells and tastes have the powerful ability to transport you back into a memory, and when they are reencountered in daily life – such as the smell of smoke returning the mind to a catastrophic house fire – a flashback is triggered.

As well as recalling the events that brought on PTSD, some flashbacks re-create the physical sensations and emotional feelings that were lived through. This is possibly due to the body's somatic memory. The brain connects all sensory feelings when storing some memories. Even if a memory hasn't been revisited for a long time, re-creating some of the sensory feelings that match a previous moment in time can cause the body to re-create multiple senses at once in the form of a flashback.

Flashbacks are essentially nightmares that occur in the awake state. However, real nightmares are also a sign of PTSD. »

> "WITH A MEMORY, YOU KNOW THE EVENT IS IN THE PAST, BUT FLASHBACKS MAKE YOU THINK THE EVENT IS HAPPENING RIGHT NOW"

COPING WITH PTSD

The chances are that every reader is familiar with a bad nightmare. The difference between general nightmares and those of PTSD sufferers are the regularity, emotional impact and percentage of the night claimed by them.

Studies suggest that 88% of war veterans experience at least one nightmare per week, due to the shocking scenes that they have been subjected to in their lives. In PTSD sufferers, the occurrence of nightmares can be much greater. Nightmares can cause people to take extreme measures to avoid falling asleep, leaving them dangerously sleep deprived.

The link between sleepless nights and post-traumatic stress disorder may be largely due to the release of the chemical serotonin in the brain while unconscious. Scientists think that the transport of serotonin is hindered in PTSD sufferers. This chemical is responsible for regulating emotions during sleep, and without it mental havoc ensues.

Just as nightmares are uncontrollable during sleep, intrusive thoughts can pop into the head of someone with PTSD without warning. These thoughts could be completely irrational, but when you have no control over your mind, you begin to accept what your brain is telling you. Commonly, they instil profound fear, blame, anger or guilt into the mind.

Because intrusive thoughts are often triggered by being in a similar place or with the same people who were there during a traumatic time, avoidance of anything associated with the memory is a core symptom of PTSD. Additionally, some people become hypervigilant regularly post-trauma. This is when the body is on high alert for danger, and for long periods. As a result, the sufferer has increased tiredness, as well as a constant theme of feeling unsafe.

With so many unsettling post-traumatic outcomes, it is understandable that some people become desperate for any form of escape from reality. Unfortunately, those who attempt this often give themselves another destructive PTSD symptom, called compulsive comfort-seeking.

Young people who have experienced traumatic abuse as children are more likely to turn to drugs and alcohol at a younger age, increasing their risk of addiction. Studies also show that, post-trauma, people are more prone to gambling, having unsafe sex and indulging in high-adrenaline activities.

The extensive list of impacts that PTSD has on the body is beneficial in helping people make sense of what they are feeling and the actions they are taking. These behaviours were once disconnected, rather than grouped together under the term PTSD. This led to misdiagnosis and misunderstanding of post-trauma mental health.

The history of PTSD
It was only in 1980 that PTSD was recognised for the true extent of its implications and causes. Back in 1688, long before it was given its name, PTSD was referred to as 'nostalgia' by a Swiss medical student called Johannes Hofer. The basis of this condition was people who complained of severe anxiety and difficulty sleeping. The term 'nostalgia' came from Hofer's other observations of homesickness and distress in soldiers in combat. Some of these early symptoms of PTSD among military patients were also recorded in other European countries, such as France and Germany.

Later, during the Civil War, PTSD symptoms were referred to as 'soldier's heart' or 'irritable heart', and in World War I it gained the widespread name 'shell shock'. These names were usually applied to all issues of pain that were beyond the capabilities of military medics' physical injury training. One of the symptoms of PTSD is a heightened nervous system,

LEARNING TO COPE

What are you supposed to do if you or a loved one develops PTSD? The first thing is to seek help, whether that is a doctor's prescribed therapy or finding a positive support group that puts you at ease. Instead of learning to avoid the aftermath of trauma, you'll cope better in the long term if you battle it head on. Relaxation techniques can assist you when you start to lose touch with reality and enter a flashback. If you know someone else who is going through PTSD, take the time to help them feel safe. You can do this by educating yourself of their triggers and making sure they know you understand their limitations. Ignoring the PTSD of other adults and children can add to their traits of avoidance and make any existing symptoms deeper-rooted.

which can result in sufferers experiencing palpitations and breathing problems.

You might wonder why the majority of history's PTSD accounts focus on soldiers in war zones. Although there are many possible causes of PTSD, analysis of soldiers helped to shine a light on these mental struggles. During events such as world wars, such a high volume of people experience trauma at one time, making the prevalence of PTSD symptoms hard to ignore.

What else can cause the disorder?

Alongside combat exposure, one of the biggest issues causing long-term PTSD is childhood abuse. This includes sexual, physical and emotional abuse. Beyond the raw trauma that these children suffer – of violence or neglect from those who are supposed to provide care during their most vulnerable years – this unfair start in life can leave children negatively impacted for many decades. For example, during the years when children grow and their identities are shaped, abuse can stunt their neurological or hormonal development. A 2021 study found that emotional abuse in particular has potential to evolve into some of the most severe cases of PTSD. All cases of child abuse increase the likelihood of PTSD, however, with more than 30% of all physical abuse, sexual abuse and neglect cases leading to lifetime PTSD.

Trust issues are a huge problem for child abuse victims, as your parents and guardians are supposed to be the first people you learn to trust. Without this basic guideline of what trust looks like, along with the incomprehensible trauma that follows this failure, some child abuse PTSD sufferers struggle to allow people close to them in their lifetime.

PTSD causes don't have to involve the let down of others. In some cases, accidents are the root cause, leaving nobody at fault. One such example is that of serious injury or illness. Being close to death, or experiencing extreme lack of physical and mental control, is traumatic for many patients following injury or illness. During the height of the Covid-19 pandemic, around 30% of those seriously affected by the virus suffered from post-Covid PTSD. Other illnesses and injuries that cause a high volume of PTSD sufferers are brain injuries, amputations, cancers and general ICU illnesses.

Dependent on each individual case, and how these incidents happened, injury-induced PTSD controls what people feel they are mentally able to do. Anybody who has sustained an injury during an activity is likely to avoid placing themselves in the same situation twice. If you swing on a chair's two legs and fall, for example, the chances are you will keep four legs firmly on the ground in the near-future. This reminder of pain is manageable, but for PTSD sufferers, who have sustained far more painful events, being in a similar scenario can trigger aggressive, painful and uncontrollable flashbacks of fearing for their life.

One of the most heartbreaking reminders of trauma comes after childbirth. Postnatal PTSD is caused by difficult labour, emergency treatment and other unexpected traumas during delivery. Because these traumatic events occur on the same day that parents welcome a new baby into their family, the baby itself can become a trigger for mothers or fathers who experienced the birth. This creates huge obstacles for parents in bonding with their babies in the earliest days, when the memories and trauma are freshest.

The pressure that surrounds new parents to make their family's new addition the happiest time of their lives means that some people struggle more to seek help. They might feel ashamed that they haven't connected with their baby, but accepting help provides the best chances of overcoming childbirth trauma and starting life as a family.

Another major trauma, which can leave people avoiding relevant locations and moments of intimacy is sexual assault. A staggering 45% of sexual assault survivors report symptoms of PTSD, including shame, detatchment and guilt. Trauma-related guilt is common across many PTSD causes, however in sexual assault it is particularly high. In some ways, this self-blame is an attempt to make a victim feel safer. By blaming themselves, victims create a false sense of fairness from the event. This might make them feel more in control, in placing the danger away from others and helping them feel safer. However, this way of thinking isn't helpful long-term and doesn't deduct from the larger emotional pain caused by PTSD.

In cases where there are no answers, or no actions that could have been taken to prevent a traumatic event, people's PTSD suffering can be extended while they struggle to comprehend »

> **EMOTIONAL ABUSE CAN EVOLVE INTO THE MOST SEVERE CASES OF PTSD**

---

5 HIGH-RISK PROFESSIONS

MILITARY
Soldiers and veterans are exposed to gruesome injuries, deaths, threats and stressful situations.

POLICE OFFICERS
These people are called to attend scenes first, with some of the most dangerous people and shocking crime scenes.

PRISON GUARDS
Prison workers are exposed to traumatic events such as prisoner suicides, self-harm and second-hand stories.

MEDICAL FIRST RESPONDERS
15-30% of these workers have PTSD, as the first to arrive at horrific disaster scenes.

JOURNALISTS
Mostly for war correspondents – this job can be high-risk for kidnappings and personal threats.

5-4-3-2-1

When in an all-absorbing PTSD flashback, one of the most popular techniques you can deploy is called grounding. Grounding involves focusing intently on something in the 'real' world, to draw yourself out of the nightmare-like state. The 5-4-3-2-1 technique is one of the best methods to follow, with the numbers making it easy to remember in times of distress. Each number focuses on a sense, and requires you to scan the surroundings using all five of them. When entering a flashback, or when any other dissociative PTSD symptom arises, all you have to do is count down from five, to speed up your return to normality. First think of, or name, five objects around you that you can see. Next, channel your attention to what your skin is in contact with and name four sensations you can feel. This can be the seat you are sitting on or the wind blowing on your neck. Thirdly, what three sounds can you hear? Even in relative silence, there could be the sound of ringing in your ears. Finally, bring yourself fully into the present with two smells and one taste.

If it seems too hard to focus on any of these five senses at first, take a moment to perform deep breathing. This will calm the overactive brain and encourage more productive focusing.

> **"THE EMOTIONAL IMPACTS OF TRAUMA ARE CONSIDERABLE, BUT PTSD PHYSICALLY ALTERS THE BRAIN AS WELL"**

the anguish. Sudden deaths of loved ones is just one of these triggers.

Our loved ones massively shape our lives, whether we see them daily, share our important thoughts with them, or just know they have got our backs. When they suddenly disappear, the emotional impact is immense. The death or disappearance of close friends and family is a cause of PTSD, especially when the loss was tragic and unforeseen.

The emotional aftermath of death is relentless enough, but imagine if intrusive thoughts left you experiencing the event on repeat, or visualising what their final moments were like in graphic detail. Generally, grief caused by PTSD lasts for at least a month, and greatly impacts someone's ability to function in daily life. After the sudden shock has lifted, however, many are able to reclaim their lives.

Why does the body hold on to the past?
It's difficult to imagine such a debilitating disorder holding a greater purpose biologically. However, the same thoughts and feelings that can be socially and emotionally crippling are in place as a survival trait.

The constant reminders of pain and the inability to relax are the brain's distorted ways to prevent you from experiencing the same harm ever again. Many of the symptoms of PTSD keep a traumatic event in the forefront of your memory, or make sure you are ready to move. Flashbacks, memories and nightmares can replay the events of your most painful days in close detail, enabling you to analyse and remember the slightest details. With this information, the body is better equipped to handle the same situation again. Although this has the potential to benefit the body physically, mentally it can feel like torture.

People who suffer from paranoia and jittery feelings, and who are constantly on the lookout, are prepared by the brain to act quickly in the face of danger. In conjunction with the emotional avoidance that limits the activities and places people can experience, those with PTSD are protecting themselves from harm but in an all-consuming way.

Although these instinctive actions make sense when explained, they are overbearing and cause more damage than advantage for someone with PTSD. For as long as this chaos is continuing in their mind, people aren't given the mental space to properly process the trauma they have encountered.

Imagine that you have endured a near-death experience, after a wave forced your head into a rock while swimming in the sea. If you encounter severe PTSD, you may experience vivid flashbacks to the extent that you can no longer go to the beach, or see a coastal scene. While this restriction does make it impossible to drown at sea, as you don't place yourself in the same situation, your strong discomfort felt at the thought of the beach disrupts your logical thought process. Being in view of the sea is no danger to you, and yet your body is acting as if it is. Once you overcome the barrier that is location association, you will be able to focus on the true danger, which in this case is overly strong waves, and the debilitating stress will disappear to improve your quality of life. Moving on from trauma can usually only happen when you face the event and accept the true causes.

Inside a traumatised brain
The symptoms of PTSD show that the emotional impacts of trauma are considerable. But, did you know that this disorder physically alters the brain as well?

Part of the brain called the hippocampus, which helps the brain to process and retrieve our memories, is smaller in the brain scans of many PTSD sufferers. In fact, a study carried out in 2011 by the University of California showed the brains of post-war veterans with PTSD to be 6% smaller than those who had recovered from it. The veterans, who fought in the 1990 Gulf War, had sustained long-term PTSD. The results from this finding can be interpreted in different ways, however. Either PTSD causes the hippocampus to shrink, but return to normal after recovery, or people with smaller hippocampuses are less likely to overcome PTSD.

A separate part of the brain, called the amygdala, is responsible for launching your body's natural alarm system. The PTSD symptoms that include being constantly on edge are caused by an overactive amygdala. The prefrontal cortex is instead underactive. This area of the brain enables you to think through every decision you make. With these two brain parts changing together, the result is that the amygdala causes PTSD sufferers to panic, while the prefrontal cortex prevents logical thinking that could limit the disorder's impact.

The fight or flight response, which creates hyperarousal in the brain, stops people from achieving calmness and contributes to feelings of anger and irritability. In turn, this stops sufferers from regulating positive emotions effectively.

How do you know if you have PTSD?
If you recognise any of the symptoms of PTSD in yourself, the best thing to do is consult a doctor. Before the diagnosis of PTSD, doctors carry out both physical and mental examinations, to deduce all possible causes of a patient's symptoms. Depending on the types and combinations of symptoms being experienced, a doctor can diagnose one of three PTSD variations.

Uncomplicated PTSD is when the disorder is caused by a single traumatic event. This is the earliest stage of PTSD and is most likely to be treated successfully. A more deep-rooted form is complex PTSD, which is diagnosed in people exposed to multiple traumatic events. This may be someone who has been sent away to fight in the army on more than one occasion, or a person who has lived long-term with an abusive partner. Considerable rage, depression or anxiety commonly feature as symptoms.

The third form of PTSD can be hidden by other health problems. Comorbid PTSD is that which exists alongside depression or another mental health concern. To cope with these strains, people with this type are most vulnerable to addiction.

Finding treatment
The worst way to cope with PTSD is alone, which is why medical professionals advise specific forms of therapy. Each of these therapies hold the same fundamental goals, tailored to individual needs. The goals are to reduce harmful symptoms, explore skills to manage symptoms and rebuild self-esteem. As well as therapy, antidepressants or anti-anxiety medications may be prescribed to lessen PTSD symptoms.

Cognitive processing therapy involves explaining, through speech and writing, exactly how a traumatic event took place. This offers a safe space to reveal in-depth thoughts and feelings. Afterwards, the therapist will explore the key issues that their patient is dwelling on. By reiterating which elements couldn't be predicted or altered, a PTSD sufferer is better able to come to terms with the series of events.

Facing your fears is one of the most productive ways to eliminate them, and prolonged exposure therapy is one method that therapists use to treat PTSD patients. Any triggers that are usually avoided are revealed for short periods, while coping strategies, such as deep breathing, are taught. The more experience the sufferer has with facing their trigger and navigating away from the trauma, the less relevance it will hold.

Not all therapy has to involve talking in-depth about uncomfortable events. Eye movement desensitisation and reprocessing (EMDR), for example, involves re-associating bad events with new and more positive feelings. While the patient concentrates their thoughts on their trauma, they also need to focus on the lights and sounds being produced by the therapist. This method is thought to store the memory differently in the brain so that the next time it emerges, it is experienced in a different way.

Mental health stigma
Since the very earliest acknowledgements of PTSD, lack of understanding has caused misconceptions of the disorder. During the Civil War, soldiers were ridiculed and branded as weak if they showed symptoms of PTSD. Some of the stigmatised views of this disorder still present today are that its sufferers are dangerous and unpredictable. This is called public stigma and can lead to self-stigma among those affected.

People who become aware of PTSD stigma may try to avoid being labelled with the disorder. This means not seeking therapy and potentially making the symptoms worse over time. If you experience any of the effects of PTSD, group therapy could be an ideal solution. Surrounded by others who understand you, you will be able to talk with others who are less likely to judge, and who empathise with what you're going through. People who attend group sessions say that it makes their story seem more valid and their problems heard.

Dealing with Intrusive Thoughts

Having an unwanted and potentially disturbing thought can be worrying, but intrusive thoughts are common. Here we explain what they are and how to manage them

WORDS JULIE BASSETT

Have you ever caught yourself thinking something unexpected or inappropriate, and wondered where that thought came from and why? For example, when you're walking on the pavement and have a fleeting thought about stepping out into the road. Or you're with a friend, whom you really like, but you wonder, for a moment, what it would be like to tip your drink over them. These are 'intrusive thoughts', which, like any form of intrusion, are unwelcome and uninvited. Depending on the nature of the thought, it can leave you feeling upset, worried, concerned or intrigued.

We all have thoughts, thousands of them, every single day. Every minute of every day in fact. One study[1] found that you might typically have more than 6,000 thoughts a day, or an average of 6.5 thoughts per waking minute. Some of these thoughts will be mundane, everyday thoughts about what you need to do that day, what you're going to eat, what you're going to wear; some will be observational, such as thinking about the weather or noticing a person you pass in the street. There are the deep thoughts that ponder on life's mysteries, your personal goals and things that worry you. Some thoughts you're very aware of, consciously making decisions or actively thinking about something. Other thoughts are subconscious, and drift in and out of your mind more freely. And then there are those intrusive thoughts, which come out of nowhere and usually are disturbing or unsettling. Most people will experience some intrusive thoughts from time to time, but for those who have them frequently, it can impact on mental health and wellbeing.

Why do we have intrusive thoughts?

Intrusive thoughts can be fairly harmless, and almost all of us experience them occasionally. They are often described as urges to do something you know you shouldn't, which could be anything from touching a button that shouldn't be touched, to stepping over the edge of a cliff when you get close. Mostly, your rational brain will kick in and wonder where that came from, but also pull you back to safety. In fact, some intrusive thoughts are so common that they have their own terminology. For example, there is the 'high »

> "INTRUSIVE THOUGHTS ARE OFTEN URGES TO DO SOMETHING YOU KNOW YOU SHOULDN'T"

MANAGE YOUR MIND 51

LEARN TO ACCEPT INTRUSIVE THOUGHTS

Most people, when they have an intrusive thought that bothers them, will try to push it away and fight against it. This can trigger more stress and worry around such thoughts, as you're teaching your brain that these thoughts are in some way harmful, and your body will react to the perceived threat. Instead, it's about learning that intrusive thoughts do not cause you harm and are not a reflection on you as a person, and you can accept them as a part of life. When you notice a thought, identify it as intrusive, remind yourself that it's just a thought, accept that it's there and then carry on with what you're doing. This teaches your brain that these thoughts are okay, allowing them to float in and out, without having an impact on the way you feel and act.

place phenomenon', which is described as the 'experience of a sudden urge to jump when in a high place'[2]. This urge to jump is found in people who have no history of suicide ideation, though it may be more common in people who are more sensitive to internal cues, and the urge to jump might actually affirm their will to live.

However, intrusive thoughts can often be far more disturbing, often violent or sexual, completely out of character for the person thinking it. This can be harder to shake off, especially when you don't understand where that thought has come from, and you wonder what it means that you've thought it. Intrusive thoughts often go against your moral, personal and spiritual beliefs, and in some people they are very upsetting. For example, parents might have a thought about hurting their child, or someone might have a thought about engaging in a sexual act with an inappropriate individual. It can be much more difficult to ignore these kinds of thoughts, especially if they come more frequently.

While most people will likely have intrusive thoughts from time to time, it does seem as though some people are more inclined towards having them more often. It's also something that can happen at any age; children and teenagers are also reported to have intrusive thoughts and they can find it harder to cope, as it's difficult for them to understand where these thoughts are coming from and how to handle them. Intrusive thoughts can be symptomatic of certain conditions; for example, those with ADHD may experience more intrusive thoughts, which can also be linked to hyperfixations. Those with OCD, who already struggle with obsessive thoughts, might also have intrusive thoughts, potentially linked to their compulsive behaviours. Persistent intrusive thoughts can indicate a mental health condition, such as anxiety or depression, or they can increase as a response to trauma, which can include flashbacks to an event. When someone is very anxious, they may experience unwanted thoughts and worries, which could be around things that are happening in their lives, or bigger worries like death. Depression can cause intrusive thoughts too, which, in more serious cases, could be around self-harm or suicide.

Intrusive thoughts can worsen as a response to lifestyle factors. For example, if you're under a lot of stress, you might find that you're more prone to these unwanted thoughts, which can be linked to what's causing your stress or might be entirely unrelated. Not getting enough sleep can be a factor, as you might find it harder to rationalise your thoughts or order them. Most intrusive thoughts pop out of nowhere in response to something you're doing, such as a sudden urge to drop a baby you're holding, or to drink a dangerous chemical you're cleaning with. However, if you're struggling in other areas of your life, and holding a lot of worry and anxiety, the frequency of these intrusive thoughts might increase.

The impact of intrusive thoughts

The impact of intrusive thoughts varies, depending on the nature and frequency of the thoughts themselves, as well as the person who is having the thoughts. For most people, when the odd thought appears, they're able to recognise it as unwanted and simply shake it off. People who are more sensitive, anxious, introspective or have a strong sense of self-awareness may notice these thoughts a lot more and ruminate on them.

If these thoughts start to come more frequently, or are particularly disturbing, the thinker may fixate on what these thoughts mean and wonder what it says about them as a person. They may then start to worry about the thoughts, causing stress and anxiety, which can then lead to even more intrusive thoughts. It may, if it progresses, even start to impact on a person's actions, causing them to change the way they behave, become over-conscious about what they say and do, or even engage in compulsive actions to try to rid themselves of these thoughts.

For those who have OCD or are highly sensitive, it can be hard to take these intrusive thoughts as just thoughts. Most of us can recognise that these thoughts are not compelling us to take action,

> **"HAVING A THOUGHT ISN'T THE SAME AS WANTING TO ACT UPON IT"**

but for others, it might prevent them from doing things, as they may regard them as a warning or believe the thought to be a truth. For example, a new parent, who is overly tired and struggling with their mental health, may experience persistent intrusive thoughts around harming their baby. This can lead them to becoming compulsive over safety measures and being overprotective, or conversely may cause them to back off from the child because they don't trust themselves around them anymore.

The problem is that the more our thoughts affect us, the more likely we are to have them. It's possible to get stuck in this intrusive thoughts cycle and it's difficult, if not impossible, to break this without outside help. If someone is struggling with frequent, persistent and disturbing intrusive thoughts, it's important to seek professional advice. Treatment usually consists of some kind of cognitive behavioural therapy (CBT) to learn how to recognise intrusive thoughts and retrain your brain to respond to them differently, to trust that these thoughts are just thoughts, and not a reflection of an actual danger.

Managing intrusive thoughts
If you're having intrusive thoughts and worried about them, even if they're only happening every so often, it's important to note that you're not alone. Most people will have them, and it is quite normal. If you find you're having them more often than usual, then you might want to look at potential lifestyle and environmental reasons as to why this is happening. Management of intrusive thoughts doesn't seek to eliminate them completely, but to help you to let thoughts come and go, without them impacting on your health and wellbeing.

Looking after your general health and wellbeing can help, as this keeps your stress levels lower and helps you to get enough rest. Make sure that you're eating a balanced diet, high in foods that are optimal for brain health, such as omega-3 fatty acids, fruits and vegetables. Drink plenty of water, and move your body regularly. It can help to ensure that you spend time outside in nature, as well as with loved ones – we feel calmer when we're more connected to the world around us. Many people also find that having a daily routine helps.

If you're going through a period of stress, make sure that you're taking time out for self-care – doing a hobby, taking part in some exercise or practising some yoga. It can also be a good idea to take a little time for meditation, ideally at the same time every day for a few minutes. Some people find journalling helpful, as you can note down any intrusive thoughts and notice if there are patterns to the type of thoughts or when you're more likely to have them.

Remember, you are not your thoughts. Having a thought isn't the same as wanting to act upon it. And intrusive thoughts are not a reflection of the type of person you are.

---

5 WAYS TO MANAGE INTRUSIVE THOUGHTS

1. RECOGNISE YOUR TRIGGERS
An increase in intrusive thoughts can often be linked to a traumatic event, grief or an increased period of stress. Understanding the root cause can make thoughts easier to manage.

2. KEEP A JOURNAL
Write down intrusive thoughts that are bothering you. Sometimes, just by recognising them in this way, you can find it easier to let them go.

3. CHALLENGE YOUR THOUGHTS
When you notice an intrusive thought, take a minute to stop and challenge it. For example, you might think, 'That's not the person I am' or 'I don't want to do that.'

4. USE MINDFULNESS
If a thought bothers you, try to ground yourself in where you are. Focus on what you can see, hear or feel to remind yourself of the present moment.

5. PRACTISE GRATITUDE
By taking time every day to focus on the things you have in your life that you're grateful for, this can help you to move on more easily from intrusive, negative thoughts.

---

[1] Tseng, J., Poppenk, J. Brain meta-state transitions demarcate thoughts across task contexts exposing the mental noise of trait neuroticism. Nat Commun, 2020
[2] Hames, Jennifer L. et al, An urge to jump affirms the urge to live: An empirical examination of the high place phenomenon, Journal of Affective Disorders, 2011

Understanding DISSOCIATIVE DISORDERS

Underdiagnosed and rarely discussed, dissociative disorders are surprisingly common, though you may not recognise them for what they are

WORDS JULIE BASSETT

The mind has many ways of coping when it's under extreme stress, whether that's due to a particular incident or traumatic experience, or as part of a mental health condition such as anxiety.

One of the ways that the mind might cope is through 'dissociation', which can leave a person feeling disconnected from their thoughts, feelings, own identity, surroundings, and/or memories.

What are dissociative disorders?
Dissociative disorders can present in several ways and for different lengths of time. Some people experience feelings of dissociation for just a few hours or days, whereas others can feel disconnected for much longer – for weeks or even months. In more extreme cases, these disorders can last many years. Symptoms vary from feelings of disconnection from yourself and your environment, to forgetting certain information or memories, and feeling unsure about who you are or having multiple identities that are distinct from each other. Some dissociative disorders can lead to feeling less or no physical pain. While dissociative disorders are mental health conditions, they lead to a range of both psychological and physical problems.

For some, these periods of dissociation are triggered by traumatic events from childhood as a way of coping; for others, they come on later in life after personal experiences that are particularly stressful or painful to process. They may be linked to other mental health conditions that increase levels of stress too. Whatever the trigger or type, dissociative disorders can be scary to experience, hard to explain and difficult to diagnose.

They are not talked about as often as other, more common, mental health conditions, and it can be a very lonely experience as a result. There are resources and services that can help, which you can see in our boxout within this feature. Thanks to people like presenter and television personality Jamie Laing openly speaking out about dissociative disorders, we can slowly begin to break the stigma surrounding these complex conditions.

The first step is in understanding what these conditions are, the signs and symptoms, and having access to the right resources and treatment.

Dissociative identity disorder
Dissociation is an umbrella term that covers different types of dissociative disorders, which have their own set of symptoms, though there is often some overlap.

You may be most familiar with a condition called dissociative identity disorder (DID), which used to be called multiple personality disorder, though that term is an older definition and a lot more is now known about the disorder. The reason you may have heard of it is because it has featured in numerous films and TV series as a plot point, using a character's »

> **"DISSOCIATIVE DISORDERS CAN BE SCARY TO EXPERIENCE AND DIFFICULT TO DIAGNOSE"**

UNDERSTANDING DISSOCIATIVE DISORDERS

UNDERSTANDING DISSOCIATIVE DISORDERS

DID to portray varying personalities to feed into the narrative. In the late '90s, *Fight Club* rose to popularity, and revealed, at its climax, that the unnamed narrator and the impulsive creator of the eponymous 'fight club' Tyler Durden were the same person.

While these cultural representations might be helpful in highlighting such mental health disorders, they are rarely accurate – DID is most often triggered by intense childhood trauma; in *Fight Club* the disorder is used to highlight the psychological trauma caused by modern materialistic culture and its trappings, to make a statement, rather than to portray the true complexities of such a condition. The same can be said of earlier cultural examples, such as *The Strange Case of Dr Jekyll and Mr Hyde*, or *Psycho*, which may contribute more to the misinformation and misunderstanding around this condition. More recently, the 2022 Marvel television series *Moon Knight* features DID central to its narrative. However, the team behind the series have said that they spent a lot of time researching DID to ensure an accurate depiction on-screen.

Having multiple distinct identities is one of the main symptoms of DID. These identities are usually identified by their own names, and can have distinct mannerisms, accents or ways of talking; they may present as different ages or genders. Each identity might have a different understanding of their own history, particularly when DID is in response to a traumatic childhood event – an identity may be created to escape from a difficult reality, omitting certain events. As such, someone with DID is likely to experience memory gaps around personal information and historical events, and feel uncertain about their own identity. Often those with DID will have an awareness of the other identities, but sometimes have an understanding of one identity that they feel is their core or 'host' identity.

It is a complex psychiatric condition, thought to be diagnosed in around 1.5% of the global population[1]. A number of people in the public eye have talked openly about their struggles with DID. Actress Roseanne Barr said in 1994 that she suffered from DID, with multiple distinct personalities. She said at the time that her DID was caused by alleged childhood abuse. Former NFL player Herschel Walker has also talked widely about his experience with DID, writing a book in 2008 called *Breaking Free: My Life with Dissociative Identity Disorder*, in which he reveals that he had a high number of alter egos, some that caused dangerous behaviours.

Other forms of dissociation
Another type of dissociative disorder is dissociative amnesia, which is when a person

GROUNDING TECHNIQUES

If you find yourself feeling disengaged with yourself or the world around you, try some of these grounding techniques to help centre yourself and feel more embedded with your reality. These can also be useful if you're feeling very stressed or anxious, or if you're suffering from a flashback. Grounding techniques use your senses to help ground you in reality.

SOUND
You may find it helpful to listen to some music that you find calming, paying attention to the lyrics to focus your attention. If you can't listen to music, then try to listen to the sounds around you instead.

TOUCH
You might want to feel something comforting, like a blanket, or find a texture in your present environment. You may wish to focus on your feet and physically ground yourself by noticing what you're standing on and pushing down to feel the ground.

BREATHING
Breathing techniques can also help. Try breathing in for four, holding for four, breathing out for four and holding for four. Or just breathing in and out slowly, but noticing each breath and its pattern.

---

[1] Mitra P, Jain A. Dissociative Identity Disorder [Updated 2022, May 17]
[2] Depersonalisation disorder: the condition you've never heard of that affects millions, The Guardian, 2015 Depersonalisation and derealisation: assessment and management, BMJ 2017;356:j745

can't remember certain personal information or events from their past. This isn't the same as being forgetful or having a bad memory, and these lapses are not linked to a medical condition or medication/treatment. It's more like certain things have been wiped from a person's memory completely, which can again be triggered by a particularly traumatic incident as a coping mechanism.

Dissociative amnesia can also cause a person to have blank episodes where they can't remember where they are or how they got there, with the condition lasting anything from a few minutes to days. In complex and rare cases, dissociative amnesia can last for many months or years, and can be combined with a state of fugue. Dissociative amnesia with fugue is when a person completely loses awareness of their own identity, and is often linked with travelling to a new location and/or with a new identity with no recollection of previous events.

Sometimes, dissociative disorders don't fit into simple categories and can be unspecified (unspecified dissociative disorder) or specified (other specified dissociative disorder). All dissociative disorders can be difficult to diagnose, and symptoms can often be attributed to other conditions before a full diagnosis is made.

Depersonalisation and derealisation
Other types of dissociative disorders are more common, and are likely to be underdiagnosed so we don't really know how many people suffer from them. Depersonalisation disorder (DPD) and derealisation disorder are two similar, but slightly different, mental health conditions that impact a greater number of people.

Depersonalisation leads to feelings of being 'outside' of yourself, as though you are observing your life and actions from a distance without feeling connected to yourself. You might also feel as if you're floating away from your body, or can't define boundaries between yourself and other people. Some people describe it as though they are watching a film about themselves.

Derealisation is when your environment feels like it's not real, and you can feel disconnected from everything around you. This can be disorienting, as objects can seem undefined and less solid.

It is possible to have depersonalisation and derealisation individually or together, and you may have a long period of disconnection, or many short periods.

It's thought that DPD could affect up to 2% of the global population, equating to over a million people in the UK (about one in 50 people) and over six million in the USA[2].

Many people don't even know that what they're experiencing is depersonalisation or derealisation, as they're not very well-known conditions.

Signs and symptoms
Given the complexity of these types of disorders, the signs and symptoms can vary hugely from person to person. Some of the symptoms present with other conditions, which is why a detailed assessment is necessary to help build a picture of the full impact of the symptoms being presented.

What makes it harder is that even those who have experienced a dissociative disorder struggle to describe their experiences. Conditions like dissociative identity disorder can, in some ways, be easier to diagnose, given the presence of distinct multiple identities. However, depersonalisation and derealisation are difficult to put into words. Those experiencing symptoms might describe their life as 'living in a dream world', or feeling 'detached' from their environment or the people around them. Other descriptions often used include the feeling that the world is 'foggy' or 'lifeless', or as a person they feel 'robotic' or watching their life from outside their body. Usually those people with these conditions are aware that what they're feeling isn't really their reality, but feel powerless to stop it from happening.

In terms of specific signs and symptoms, there are some to be aware of that may point towards a dissociative disorder. This can include things like having blank periods in your life around certain events, or gaps in your memory, including personal

> "IT CAN BE HARD TO EXPLAIN HOW YOU'RE FEELING"

information. You may find yourself in a strange or different location, with no recollection of how you got there. You may have a sensation that the world around you isn't quite real, and that objects and places seem to change and distort. You might feel robotic or lifeless, or feel like the world is blurred or foggy. You may feel detached from your reality and environment, or from your own body, like you're watching your life from the outside. You may be disconnected from your sense of identity, or notice that other identities are present. This can make it very difficult to define who you are, which can be confusing and overwhelming.

Getting a diagnosis
A family doctor or GP is the first port of call if you're worried that you have the symptoms of a dissociative disorder. It can be hard to explain how you're feeling, so it's worth writing down any episodes you can remember, or thoughts you are struggling with. Accounts of many episodes and occurrences can help to build a picture for the doctor to help diagnose these conditions.

First, a doctor will need to rule out other causes for the symptoms. Certain drugs »

or medications, for example, can cause dissociation, as can alcohol misuse. There could be a physical cause for the feelings of dissociation, such as a head injury, or another condition, such as anxiety. If there is no clear cause, then a full mental health assessment is likely to be conducted, ideally via a psychotherapist or psychiatrist with a background in dissociative disorders.

This assessment requires honesty to get a reliable diagnosis. It may be that the symptoms are more likely to be linked to another mental health condition, and the way the episodes impact on your everyday life will be taken into consideration too. It can still be difficult to get diagnosed with a dissociative disorder, partly due to an overlap in symptoms with more common mental health conditions; partly due to a lack of understanding of these conditions; and partly due to the difficulty in describing the symptoms.

Not everyone finds a specific diagnosis helpful, particularly if the symptoms are short-lived, infrequent or don't have a huge impact on your day-to-day life. In these cases, self-help and online resources can be useful, and you can still ask for help with your symptoms, even without a formal diagnosis. It might be that you come across dissociative disorders as a result of your own research and readings, trying to make sense of the way you feel and what you're experiencing.

What causes dissociative disorders?
Dissociative disorders often come about due to a specific trauma, though not everyone who experiences a difficult or traumatic event will experience dissociation.

These disorders are more likely in those who experience some form of abuse or neglect, particularly at a young age or over a long period of time. The younger a person is when they experience trauma, the more likely dissociation is, as the young mind cannot cope with processing what is happening to them. More extreme cases of dissociation are often triggered by childhood experiences like physical, sexual or emotional abuse, or severe neglect, when dissociation is the only way that child can remove themselves from a situation. Dissociation is also more likely to occur if a child doesn't have a source of comfort or support in their life during a difficult time, or if the neglect or abuse is caused by someone they are emotionally attached to. It also means that, as an adult, that person doesn't have any other mechanisms to cope with stress and will dissociate during difficult periods.

Other causes and risk factors are one-off incidents of extreme trauma as adults that can't be processed in any other way. It's normal to dissociate during the initial traumatic event as a way of coping and to protect the mind. The problem occurs when dissociation continues for a long time afterwards and it can become a coping mechanism for everyday stresses too. When linked to a particularly traumatic event, your mind may block out certain memories. However, something can trigger these memories and cause flashbacks, which can be very difficult to cope with, especially if the memory has been repressed for a long time.

Depersonalisation and derealisation are not always caused by a specific trauma or event, and can happen alongside other mental health conditions that put the body in a state of stress.

No one is really sure why we experience dissociation when stressed or traumatised. In difficult situations, the mind goes into 'fight' or 'flight' mode, and this is relatively well understood. Dissociation might occur when neither of these options are viable, when you can't escape or fight a situation, as a way of protecting you from what you're

SUPPORT SOMEONE WITH A DISSOCIATIVE DISORDER

It can be really hard if someone you care for is experiencing a dissociative disorder. There are some practical things that you can do to support them, such as help them to get the treatment or therapy they need. That might be booking a doctor's appointment to discuss options, finding a good therapist or helping them make a crisis plan for periods of dissociation. They may need someone they trust to act as an advocate for them, especially as dissociative disorders can be hard to diagnose. You can also aid them to stay safe during an episode, by understanding their triggers and helping them to avoid them or navigate them. They may also need to talk about what they are going through, and you can listen, even if you can't do anything.

Dissociative disorders can be hard on friends and family, especially if someone you care for is exhibiting different identities, or has long periods of dissociative amnesia. Make sure that you look after your own wellbeing, as you will find it hard to support them if you are burnt out yourself. Get adequate rest and sleep, engage with support groups to talk with others who are going through a similar experience, and ask for extra help if you need to.

UNDERSTANDING DISSOCIATIVE DISORDERS

> ❝ DISSOCIATIVE DISORDERS OFTEN COME ABOUT DUE TO A SPECIFIC TRAUMA ❞

experiencing. Dissociation may stop us forming solid memories or understanding where we are or what is happening, changing the way we think and feel until the real or perceived trauma has passed. This would explain periods of amnesia, or sensations of detachment and unreality.

Links to other conditions

Dissociative disorders can appear on their own, or alongside another mental health condition. This is why it can be hard to define a dissociative disorder and it's not uncommon to get a diagnosis of a different condition instead.

When dissociation is triggered by a specific traumatic event, a person may also suffer from post-traumatic stress disorder (PTSD). This causes a person to relive a traumatic event and suffer from flashbacks. PTSD is thought to affect one in three people who experience trauma, and can be more likely if the trauma is experienced in childhood and/or over a sustained period of time.

Depersonalisation or derealisation can be experienced by people who also suffer from anxiety and panic attacks. The panic attacks can convince the mind that it is undergoing a traumatic event and the mind reacts to the perceived threat just as it would a real one. Long-term anxiety can build up and create a lot of stress in the body, which can trigger dissociation to escape the situation. Depression, phobias, insomnia and obsessive compulsive disorder (OCD) can also create situations where the mind is over-stressed and triggers a dissociation episode.

If a person suffers from a dissociative disorder for a long period of time, this can also lead to thoughts of self-harm or suicidal tendencies, as they struggle to connect with themselves or the world around them.

Treatment and self-care

Once a dissociative disorder has been recognised or diagnosed, there are treatments available. For many people, this will be in the form of a talking therapy, such as counselling. This gives you the space to talk through how you are feeling and to face the causes of stress in your mind and body.

This might be specific trauma counselling, which can be very difficult, but sometimes by facing the trauma in a safe environment and being given the chance to confront it can help to relieve the symptoms of dissociation.

For those who experience depersonalisation or derealisation linked to anxiety, depression or panic attacks, learning techniques to help cope with periods of disconnection can make dissociative episodes easier to manage. We have covered some ideas for grounding techniques in the box on page 56, which are things you can do in the moment if you feel disconnected or disengaged from the world around you or from yourself.

Many people find that the right counselling is enough to recover from a dissociative disorder, especially if the underlying cause or trigger is addressed and coping mechanisms and techniques are learned.

There are some medications that are used, however there is nothing specifically for dissociative disorders. Rather, there are medications that can help to treat triggers, causes and other symptoms that might then help with the dissociation. For example, being unable to sleep (insomnia) can make dissociation harder to cope with, so medication might be prescribed to help. Anti-depressants can also be used to manage depression or anxiety when present alongside dissociation.

There are also some self-help techniques that can be useful. Some people find that keeping a journal helps, writing down your thoughts and feelings so that you become more aware of them. For people with DID, this can help to connect different identities, and for those who experience periods of amnesia, a diary can help with memory gaps. Other tips include writing notes for yourself with useful information, such as the time and date, emergency contact numbers and reminders, so that if your dissociation causes memory blanks or conflicting identities, you have a practical reference.

It's also important to look after yourself in other ways. The fundamentals of a healthy life can help you to cope better with a dissociative disorder, such as eating a balanced diet, getting enough sleep and doing some exercise. These things help to manage your mental health and wellbeing, which in turn can help with dissociative disorders.

If you are worried about yourself, a friend or a loved one suffering from a dissociative disorder, then please refer to the useful resources, tips and links in the boxes throughout this feature.

ESSENTIAL RESOURCES AND LINKS

UK

Mind
mind.org.uk
Mind Infoline 0300 123 3393
(Monday-Friday, 9am-6pm)

Samaritans
samaritans.org
Call 116 123 (24/7)

Clinic for Dissociative Studies
www.clinicds.co.uk

European Society for Trauma and Dissociation
www.estd.org

First Person Plural
www.firstpersonplural.org.uk

SHOUT
giveusashout.org
Text 'Shout' 85258 (24/7)

USA

National Alliance on Mental Illness (NAMI)
www.nami.org
Helpline 1-800-950-NAMI (6264)

988 Suicide & Crisis Lifeline:
https://988lifeline.org
Call 988 (24/7)

Crisis Text Line
www.crisistextline.org
Text 'Home' 741741 (24/7)

Sidran Institute (Traumatic Stress Education & Advocacy)
www.sidran.org

AUSTRALIA

Samaritans
thesamaritans.org.au
Call 135 247 (8am-8pm)

Lifeline
www.lifeline.org.au
Call 13 11 14 (24/7) Text 0477 13 11 14

Suicide Call Back Service
www.suicidecallbackservice.org.au
1300 659 467

SANE
www.sane.org
Call 1800 187 263

ReachOut.com (for young people)
https://au.reachout.com/

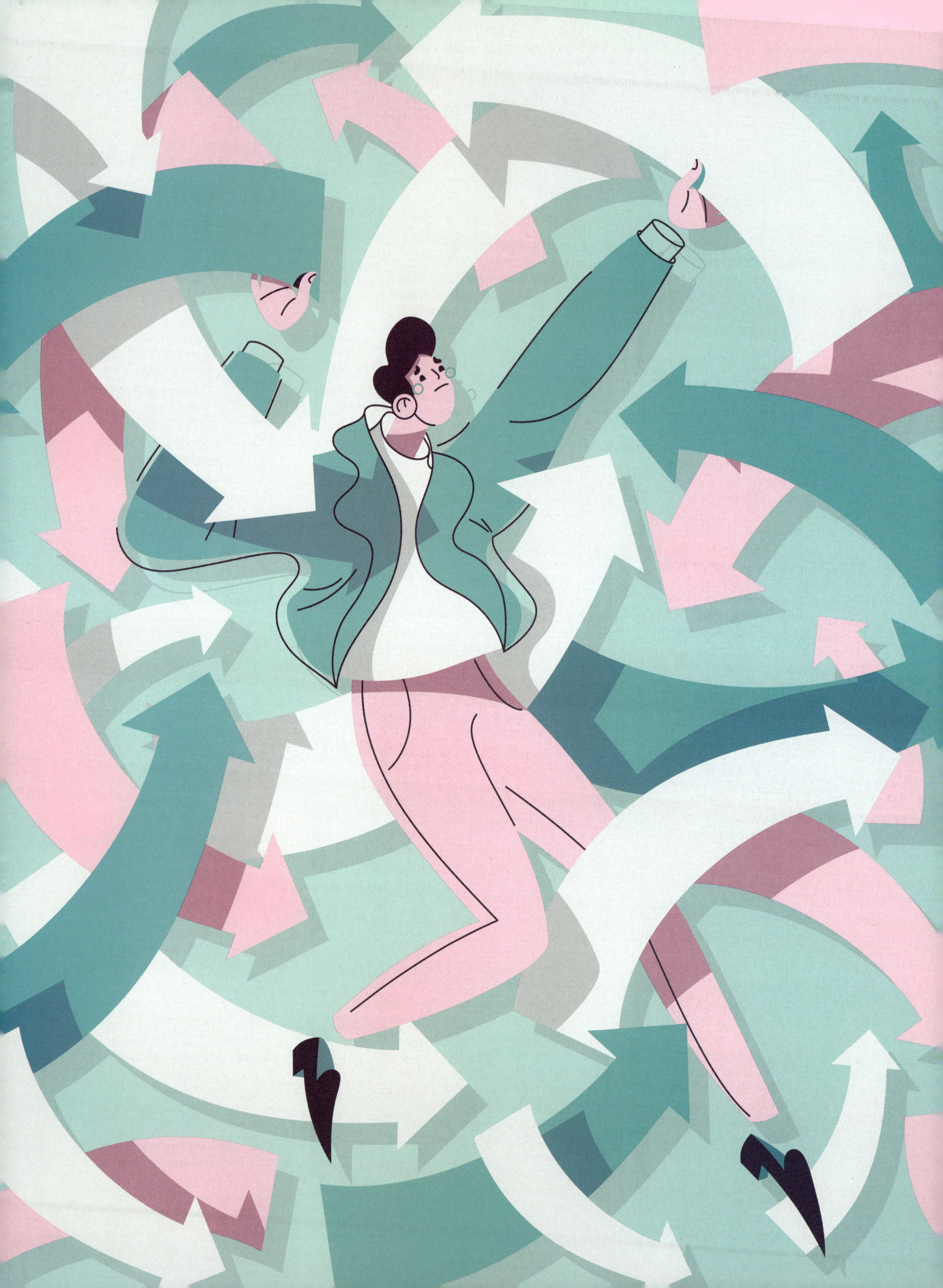

LIVING WITH ADHD

Living
WITH ADHD

Explore the remarkable struggles and strengths dictated by this disorder

WORDS AILSA HARVEY

Attention deficit/hyperactivity disorder (ADHD) is a neurodevelopmental condition recognised by a person's inability to focus, control impulses, organise efficiently or plan ahead. It is one of the most common neurodevelopmental conditions, and yet diagnoses are often missed and people with it misunderstood. As people come to understand and accept neurodivergence in society, and the stigma surrounding it becomes less, the number of people receiving an ADHD diagnosis is growing. Over the last eight years, there have been 42% more ADHD diagnoses.

Not everybody experiences ADHD in the same way, and there are three main types. The first is inattentive ADHD, causing someone to become easily distracted from a task or conversation. A person with inattentive ADHD can seem relatively calm to an outsider, but is battling the brain's tendency to take diverging trains of thought. Contrastingly, someone with the hyperactive-impulsive type could be constantly fidgeting in any given situation, or chatting away with an abundance of energy. This type is more common in males than females.

The third type is called combination ADHD and means that the person diagnosed can't be exclusively described as having mostly inattentiveness or hyperactivity. A combination of the two symptoms are exhibited in these people, and the ADHD can present itself differently in each scenario. Each type isn't fixed, as a person can change their behaviour slowly over time, shifting to become more or less hyperactive or focused.

What are the main signs?
Although not being able to focus is one of the primary signs of ADHD, this isn't a trait limited to someone with the disorder. Most people share this feeling throughout life, when the brain is experiencing periods of tiredness and stress. However, just because you zone out in the classroom or notice some reluctance to get started with a piece of work doesn't necessarily mean you have ADHD. So, when should you be wary of these signs?

The difference between standard concentration fluctuations and those of someone with the disorder is the severity and resulting impact on life events. For example, if you begin to daydream during a conversation, this can be embarrassing. Someone who just does this occasionally may notice that they haven't been taking in the information someone is telling them, and can immediately tune back in when they actively try to. Those with ADHD however, might lose focus more easily. This includes struggling to continue with a repetitive task for more than a few minutes, and frequently spacing out of conversations without realising or being able to easily return to concentration. Occasionally losing focus is normal and becomes a minor inconvenience, while ADHD-related inattention causes significant issues in daily life.

There are a range of ways in which ADHD can present itself, depending on a person's type of disorder and lifestyle activities. Typically, these signs emerge when a person is between ages three and »

> **"NOT EVERYBODY EXPERIENCES ADHD IN THE SAME WAY, AND THERE ARE THREE MAIN TYPES"**

MANAGE YOUR MIND

six, but many people have been classed as disruptive, thought to be choosing to act out or not given the necessary attention. As a result, they only receive their ADHD diagnosis as adults.

The brain of someone with inattentive ADHD enables them to experience boredom more quickly than others. When presented with new information, they may be unable to take it in or organise their thoughts. This can present itself in navigational situations. Even if someone has just relayed a small series of directions, the brain is unable to process and recall the steps, preventing them from following the directions.

Signs of having more hyperactive and impulsive ADHD include finding it difficult to sit in silence without talking, or remaining still without fidgeting. In addition, a person may say or do something as soon as they have a thought, without much consideration of the consequences of their actions.

The power of diagnosis

Males are around three times more likely to be diagnosed with ADHD than females. Not only is this due to the higher prevalence of ADHD in males, but it is also due to the type of ADHD that is more common in males and females. Females are more likely to have inattentive ADHD and may not show the more outwardly obvious signs of being hyperactive. People experiencing symptoms of ADHD before the mid-1990s were less likely to be diagnosed by specialists if they were female or weren't hyperactive. Many of these people are diagnosed with ADHD as adults.

A diagnosis can be extremely eye-opening for adults, leading to them better understanding themselves and aspects of their behaviour they may have been ashamed of before – or even shamed by others for. When ADHD isn't diagnosed during childhood, people grow up thinking they are badly behaved and there is no way to control it. In reality, their brains just function differently to others around them. Without the extra support and understanding of the disorder, adults with ADHD can grow up with low self-esteem and feel as though they lack control. Being told to "do better" while at school, but not being given the support needed to do so, these feelings of not being good enough can become internalised. As a result of limited control, undiagnosed individuals are more likely to suffer from anxiety or depression.

Receiving a late diagnosis isn't always relieving. For some people this triggers feelings of sadness and anger. People often ask themselves 'Why?' and 'What if…?' Periods of their life that have been impacted by undiagnosed ADHD, such as relationship difficulties, failure at school or other lost opportunities, could have been improved or avoided with treatment and better understanding. In some aspects, diagnosis brings some feelings of grief.

When children's ADHD is identified early in life, teachers are able to tailor their learning to optimise their chances of success. This includes arranging seating plans in rows for limited distractions, taking care to repeat instructions and not shaming children for missing those already explained, teaching with visual tools and finding ways to make organisation simpler. Ultimately, one system doesn't work for every child. The more information teachers are provided about a child, the more options they can be given for learning. This helps them to know what works for them, and provides them with successful tools they can use for the rest of their lives. Today, there is increasingly more awareness of ADHD, and so diagnoses are easier to obtain. With the right support, children are receiving better education for their needs.

ADHD was renamed from ADD (attention deficit disorder) to ADHD in 1987 to recognise that hyperactivity is a core symptom of the disorder. This led to some people feeling that they were labelled inaccurately, as it gave the impression that all those with ADHD had high energy. Now ADHD is used to refer to those who experience either or both of the symptoms and is written with a slash between words to highlight this (attention deficit/hyperactivity disorder).

ADHD and the brain

What exactly is going on in the brain to cause disruption in a person's train of thought and concentration? The main difference between the brain of a child with ADHD and one without is the size of the frontal lobe. This is the area at the front of the brain, behind the forehead, which can mature later in people with ADHD. The frontal lobe is responsible for

SECURING SLEEP

People with ADHD usually sleep for shorter periods at a time and struggle to get to sleep. For anyone who has had difficulties sleeping, the following day can be a long struggle. This includes dragging yourself out of bed with sore eyes and hours of daytime sleepiness. The type of ADHD a person has impacts the cause of sleep deprivation. Inattentive ADHD prevents a person from going to bed at their desired bedtime. Due to shortening a person's attention span, someone with this form of ADHD can find multiple new activities to begin while carrying out their nighttime routine. Someone with more hyperactive ADHD symptoms is more likely to experience insomnia when in bed.

To achieve a smoother sleeping routine, it can help some people with ADHD to only go to bed when feeling tired. Before this time, you are more likely to lie awake and grow increasingly agitated. You can also avoid using screens before bed and any activities that you know you might fixate on. Try to keep a consistent bedtime schedule and any tasks you feel an urge to complete could be made into a to-do list. Doing this sets them aside for a designated time and can help you to feel like you have started to organise them.

> **"A LATE ADHD DIAGNOSIS CAN BE A RELIEF, OR IT CAN TRIGGER ANGER AND SADNESS"**

organising, planning, attention, impulse control and decision making.

Part of the brain within the frontal lobe, called the prefrontal cortex, regulates a person's thoughts, actions and emotions. To receive information and deliver it around the brain for processing, the brain sends signals across neurons. Studies suggest that in the brains of individuals with ADHD, there are fewer neurotransmitters activated between the prefrontal cortex and the basal ganglia, nearer the centre of the brain. As a result, there is less dopamine released, a neurotransmitter that interacts with other neurotransmitters to regulate mood. If a person has less dopamine activity, they need other ways to fulfil the feeling of reward that dopamine gives the brain.

ADHD brains are therefore chemically wired to seek more dopamine. Some of the activities people may regularly engage in are playing video games and exercising. Being physically active can regulate the symptoms of ADHD and help make a person with the disorder feel more engaged and organised in daily life. Dopamine in the body works to regulate impulse control, so if the levels are low, you can expect to have higher impulsivity.

Other areas of mental function that the prefrontal cortex regulates are alertness, attention span and short-term memory. There is still so much that scientists are working to uncover about the function of ADHD brains. However, by recognising the imbalance of neurotransmitters in the brain, people are able to begin to understand why they think and behave the way they do.

Can it be controlled?

If you have been diagnosed with ADHD, the next step is to find methods of controlling the symptoms in ways that can enhance your lifestyle and enable you to achieve any ambitions. As an adult, some of the essential, mundane chores can quickly become overwhelming if you have ADHD. There is so much to focus on at once, from bill paying and home organisation to relationships and jobs.

The solutions to managing ADHD symptoms involve both lifestyle techniques and prescribed medication. One of the greatest challenges to tackle with the disorder is how to stay organised. While other people may be able to focus on one goal – to tidy the house – it might be better for someone with ADHD to break down this task into sub-tasks. If you start on one big project, to sort out all aspects of the home at once, the task becomes more daunting and you are then more likely to become distracted. If you have a list of »

5 SUCCESSFUL PEOPLE WITH ADHD

RICHARD BRANSON
The entrepreneur co-founded the Virgin Group in the 1970s. Speaking publicly about his ADHD, he said, "If I feel I've learnt all there is about something, I want to move on and learn about something else. As a result, I've created 500 different companies in my lifetime."

MICHAEL PHELPS
Olympic swimmer Michael Phelps was diagnosed with ADHD as a child and struggled to focus at school. Phelps had high hyperactivity, but learned how to channel this energy into his swimming training, gaining him 23 Olympic gold medals for the USA.

GRETA GERWIG
Gerwig is an American actor, director and screenwriter, who directed the films *Barbie*, *Little Women* and *Lady Bird*. Speaking about her ADHD diagnosis, she said, "I've always had a tremendous amount of enthusiasm. I was just interested in everything."

JIM CARREY
The famous actor and comedian was diagnosed with ADHD. In school he would disrupt other children after finishing his work. However, in the right environment – on stage and screen – Carrey channelled his energy and creativity to become hugely successful.

LILY ALLEN
In 2022, the British singer revealed her ADHD diagnosis and explained how this led to her changing her lifestyle habits. She said, "I've had to completely switch off social media, because as soon as I look at it, it can be hours of my day gone."

THE AUTISM CORRELATION

ADHD and autism are two of the most common neurodevelopmental disorders, and share some symptoms, such as impulsivity and difficulty focusing and communicating. Because of this, the two can be confused. However, the disorders often occur at the same time, with 28-44% of people with autism also having ADHD.

When it comes to situations that require focus, a person with ADHD and one with autism can struggle, but for different reasons. The differences can be spotted in children. Autistic individuals may be unable to focus on an activity if it is one they don't particularly enjoy, but can fixate for long periods on their interests. People with ADHD are likely to dislike an activity if they need to concentrate on it.

Studies show that if a child is diagnosed with both conditions, they are more likely to show signs of combined ADHD, expressing hyperactivity and impulsivity, while struggling to pay attention. When ADHD and autism meet, an individual can experience an internal conflict between wanting to be impulsive while striving for a comforting, structured routine.

> "DOING ACTIVITIES AT THE SAME TIME EVERY DAY HELPS BUILD HABITS AND REDUCES PROCRASTINATION"

small steps, such as 'cleaning the bookshelf' or 'hanging up clothes', then each task is shorter and can be ticked off the list more easily. This gives you a clearer vision of what has been done and a more systematic approach. Physically ticking a to-do list also releases dopamine into the body, helping to keep you on-task. Furthermore, if you get distracted, you can return to the list for guidance. Knowing what to prioritise may reduce the impulsivity to switch activities.

Calendars and planners are a vital tool for many people with ADHD, to manage appointments and stay on top of deadlines. Opting for a digital version of each can assist you further, as you can set automatic reminders. This automation adds more guidance and structure that you don't have to depend on your memory for.

To assist lifestyle tweaks, there are also five medication options that can be prescribed by a doctor to manage the symptoms of ADHD. These don't cure ADHD but can help to improve the mindset of some with the disorder. The five types of medicine are called methylphenidate, lisdexamfetamine, dexamfetamine, atomoxetine and guanfacine.

Methylphenidate is a stimulant and the most common of the five. To treat ADHD, the medicine increases activity in the brain to improve attention. Adults and children over five years old can take these tablets daily to enhance concentration. Lisdexamfetamine is given to people who don't show signs of behavioural improvement after six weeks on methylphenidate. It is considered more effective but is also more likely to cause side effects, such as weight loss, nausea and decreased appetite. When lisdexamfetamine is absorbed into the bloodstream, and comes into contact with red blood cells, it is converted into its active form. It then increases dopamine levels in the nervous system. Dexamfetamine works in the same way as lisdexamfetamine.

Atomoxetine is a medication that works to control impulses and concentration by producing more signals between brain cells. To do this, the medication increases the amount of a chemical called noradrenaline in the brain. This is the chemical responsible for passing messages between neurons. Finally, guanfacine stimulates the part of the brain responsible for controlling attention spans and strengthens the neuron network in this area. This medication has also proven to reduce blood pressure. For all of these medications, you should speak with your doctor so that you are aware of all the possible side effects.

Supporting a child

Raising a child with ADHD can be daunting. Unlike other aspects of their life, which you have first-hand experience of, you may not have a brain that works in the same way as theirs. The best way to support them is to become well-educated on the signs and implications of ADHD. This will help you to be understanding. Many of the behaviours a child with ADHD exhibits aren't entirely controlled by the child, so becoming angry can make them feel unseen, isolated and frustrated.

When speaking to a child with ADHD you should aim to give any instructions when they are looking at you. This increases the chance that you have gained their attention and what you are saying is being heard. Remember not to set extended tasks and instead break up a routine into smaller and more manageable activities.

If there are other people in the family, the best way to handle life with ADHD is to not ignore it or overly focus your attention on the disorder. This means that you should explain the difference in needs to other siblings, but don't focus too much of your attention on just the child with ADHD. This can make them feel singled out. All children will benefit from a regular routine and exercise. Make sure bedtime is set and remains consistent every night. Before bedtime, remove screens and promote relaxing activities to limit energy spikes or distractions.

Lastly, it is important to focus on the child's strengths as well as their challenges. ADHD can increase a person's enthusiasm for topics and activities. Give regular praise to your child when deserved, while also having clear boundaries. This lets a child know that you recognise their difficulties without letting them get away with damaging impulsive behaviour. They will grow up to celebrate themselves and their own personal achievements and learn that violence or disorderly behaviour won't be accepted as an outlet for their struggles. If your child is acting out a lot, try to create a safe space where you can communicate with them about their feelings. ADHD can make it more difficult for people to manage their emotions, so it is vital they can disclose this with you or a specialist to get any additional help they need.

Navigating the workplace with ADHD

Some of the skills that employers search for in their workforce include those that someone with ADHD has to input more effort to achieve. In an office job, for example, people are required to work sitting still for hours at a time, while surrounding colleagues create a multitude of potential distractions. Most people without ADHD could tune out from the background noises and movements, while someone with the disorder will divert their attention much more easily. In addition, employees are often expected to manage their time, stay on top of multiple projects, meet strict deadlines and pay attention to new information.

Work can take up a significant portion of your life, so it is good to experiment with strategies to optimise your comfort and performance in the workplace. Firstly, prioritise a new morning routine for your job. Punctuality can be a challenge with an easily distracted mind, but with added structure you can work on controlling your impulses. Doing activities at the same time every day helps build habits and reduces the likelihood of procrastination.

When at work, if you find yourself unable to remember information from meetings, take a pen and paper with you. Even if you are the odd one out in today's increasingly digital world, physically writing information down has been proven more effective for recalling it later by increasing brain activity.

If your working environment allows it, attempt to declutter the space around you. The fewer distractions in your eyeline, the less your ADHD will steal your focus. Playing white noise or calming music while working works similarly to block out audible distractions.

Another useful technique, if you are concerned about your perception or communication skills, is to actively seek feedback. Having regular one-on-one meetings with your colleagues and boss can help you to understand each other. Ask for constructive criticism on your work ethic and communication skills, and be honest about your disorder. This will prevent any misunderstandings and keep you on track with your targets.

How does ADHD affect relationships?

ADHD can make a person enthusiastic, intriguing and exciting to be around. So many unique and desirable traits can be influenced by the disorder and make a person loveable. But oftentimes, the best part of a person comes alongside more challenging attributes. Close relationships bring hurdles for both the person with ADHD and the person in a relationship with them.

Navigating the extra stresses of daily life with ADHD can increase a person's anxiety. By the end of the day, when at home with their partner, it might only take a small comment or action to release the frustration. In this situation, both people in the couple need to learn to recognise when stress is building. Instead of tentatively avoiding an outburst, open and calm conversations need to be had to diffuse negative emotions.

The impulsive side of some people with ADHD can result in relationships forming very quickly. When entering a relationship this way, built on initial feelings, the connection may fade quickly as it is less likely to be built on each other's needs. Part of this is due to the person with ADHD overthinking the situation or losing interest. To overcome the chances of this situation, if a relationship develops quickly, both people should communicate openly what they are looking for in the relationship and be honest with each other about feelings. This helps the person with ADHD to gain security and think through whether the situation is suitable for both.

The most important attribute for all in a relationship to master is understanding. For the person without ADHD, there are many occasions that could lead to them feeling underappreciated. This includes forgetting appointments in the calendar, accidentally zoning out mid-conversation and getting bored easily. However, the more you learn about your partner's disorder, the more knowledgeable you will become about how their brain works.

The beauty of ADHD

ADHD stays with a person for life. But, with experience it becomes easier to manage. At times when the symptoms become overwhelming to manage, it is worth acknowledging the aspects of the disorder that contribute to some of the best qualities in a person's personality.

If you have ADHD, your ability to hyperfocus on one thing at a time can lead to you excelling at something far quicker than others around you. This builds highly talented individuals and some of the most successful people on the planet. ADHD also makes many people more creative, enthusiastic and funny. They are often the most popular people in a room due to their vibrant exterior. In addition, being forced to work harder than others around you for some aspects of school and general life can be the making of a persistent and empathetic individual.

The more awareness there is around the thought processes of those with ADHD, the more freedom there is for neurodivergent people to be themselves, understand their most desirable and challenging qualities, and find a place of support that they need to reach their true potential.

WHY WE GET ADDICTED

WHY WE GET *Addicted*

Discover how our brains can be tricked into wanting more and more

WORDS SCOTT DUTFIELD

Addiction is a biopsychosocial disorder, meaning that its occurrence is a combination of a person's biology, mental health and societal factors. It's typically associated with a dependency on different harmful substances or behaviours, such as the use of narcotics, alcohol or gambling, but can also apply to overdoing anything that leads to harm.

What unites addictions is their ability to increase the levels of dopamine in the body. Dopamine is a neurotransmitter that's made in the brain. When it's released, it activates the nucleus accumbens, also known as the pleasure centre of the brain. Outside of addiction, dopamine is released during pleasurable experiences, such as getting food, watching a film or anything that brings you joy. However, this built-in reward system can be hijacked by other substances and damaging behaviours.

Some substances, such as heroin, marijuana and nicotine, mimic the presence of a chemical messenger that activates nerve cells called neurons. When activated, neurons generate electrical signals to tell the brain to release dopamine. Other substances, like cocaine or amphetamines, flood the dopamine system and cause it to release abnormally large amounts of neurotransmitters. They also disrupt the cycling of dopamine to make its presence last longer. These drugs can trigger the release of between two and ten times the amount of dopamine that is naturally produced from normal pleasurable experiences, such as eating food.

The point at which we become addicted is when our brains adapt to the presence of this excess dopamine. When that excess is missing, the body craves it. When the body experiences these false 'hits' of dopamine, over time it will begin to start reducing the level of naturally produced dopamine and

> **"WE BECOME ADDICTED WHEN OUR BRAINS ADAPT TO THE PRESENCE OF EXCESS DOPAMINE"**

also reduce the number of dopamine receptors. With low natural production of dopamine and a decrease in the number of receptors cycling it, addicted individuals will continue to use a substance or engage in behaviours that bring the brain to its newly adapted dopamine levels.

Coffee addicts

You might be an addict without actually realising it. In the Western world, more than 80% of humans ingest caffeine on a regular basis in amounts that are large enough to affect their brains. Caffeine is a psychoactive stimulant that affects the same part of the brain as cocaine, but in a very different way. It mostly enhances concentration and improves mood, but it creates a surge in dopamine similar to other addictive drugs, but on a much smaller scale. Caffeine drinkers also experience an increase in their tolerance, meaning the more coffee they drink, the more they need in order to receive the same energising results.

Like any other drug, the removal of caffeine-packed coffee will result in the body experiencing withdrawal, symptoms of which include headaches, fatigue and decreased motivation. However, unlike other more destructive drugs, studies have shown that quitting caffeine is much more easily achieved than quitting substances like cocaine.

Infinite scroll

It remains unclear how addictive social media is, but since the invention of the infinite scroll in 2006, social media platforms are making it harder for you to quit. The infinite scroll was invented to allow users of a social media platform to scroll down through content seamlessly and endlessly instead of clicking at the bottom of a page for more content. The switch to infinite scroll means that we're always anticipating the next piece of content, causing dopamine levels to slightly spike and then quickly fall when the next piece of content is revealed. This dopamine system will continue until you make the active choice to shut down social media or your phone's battery runs out.

THE SCIENCE OF SMOKING

After just one puff, nicotine can get its claws into you

NICOTINE
This stimulant alkaloid is found in the nightshade family of plants, including tobacco.

→ **NEURON**
Nicotine interacts with neurons, which in turn send signals to the brain to release dopamine.

→ **FALSE SIGNAL**
When nicotine enters the neuron it imitates a neurotransmitter called acetylcholine, causing the neuron to create an electrical signal in the brain.

→ **DOPAMINE**
When released, this neurotransmitter activates part of the brain associated with experiencing pleasure.

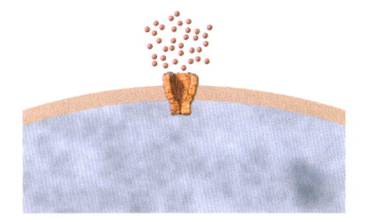

NORMAL LEVELS
Without the presence of nicotine, neurons operate normally, activated by a type of neurotransmitter called acetylcholine.

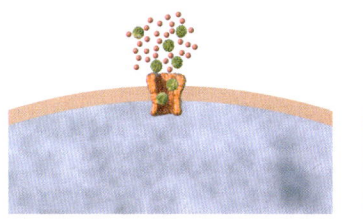

NICOTINE RUSH
Within the first few seconds of inhaling the smoke of a cigarette, nicotine binds to neuron receptors that normally bind with acetylcholine.

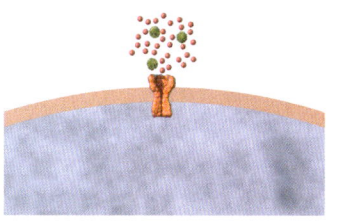

BURNT OUT
Once nicotine has been used up and is no longer present, receptors return to normal function.

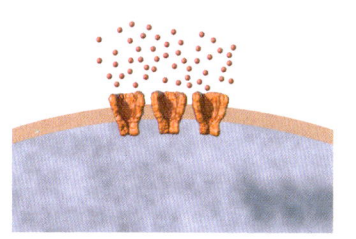

ADDICTION
At the point of addiction, neuron receptors wait for the arrival of nicotine and the body craves the resulting rush of dopamine.

COPING WITH *Catastrophic* THOUGHTS

It starts with a flicker of worry, but your brain starts imagining numerous different devastating outcomes… what is catastrophising and what can we do about it?

WORDS JULIE BASSETT

Do you always tend to focus on the worst-case scenario? Play a game of 'what if?', moving from one terrifying possibility to another?

This type of negative mindset is known as 'catastrophising', characterised by a tendency to focus on the worst possible result to any situation. It doesn't usually start out with complete catastrophe; often the initial worry can be small and proportionate. For example, if you make an error at work, you might legitimately be concerned about how to correct the mistake and explain it to your manager. And then you might ruminate on it, creating scenarios in your mind where you get in trouble for the error, are called into a meeting, lose your job and then struggle to pay your bills, leaving you in a desperate situation. You can get caught in a spiral, with each thought progressively worse than the one before, until you land on complete catastrophe.

Understanding catastrophising

Catastrophising falls under the umbrella term of 'cognitive distortion', which refers to exaggerated and negative ways of thinking. As well as catastrophising, cognitive distortions cover things like jumping to – and responding to – wrong conclusions, punishing yourself for situations that are out of your control, and blaming others for the way you feel, among others. Catastrophising is not a diagnosable mental health condition in itself, but those who struggle with their mental health are more susceptible to cognitive distortions, irrational thought patterns and negative thinking. It is more often experienced by those with general anxiety, panic disorder, social anxiety and obsessive compulsive disorder. Those who are under a lot of stress may also be more prone to catastrophising, as well as those who have gone through a traumatic event or a period of grief.

If you experience catastrophising, it can feel exhausting. Your body will respond to the perceived crisis, which can manifest both mentally and physically. You might feel emotional, your heart may begin racing, you may feel hot or dizzy, and you might get headaches or other pains. And if this pattern of thinking becomes more frequent, it can begin to have a huge knock-on effect on your mental wellbeing, leading to increased stress levels, anxiety and depression. Catastrophising is something that can impact anyone of any age; children and teenagers might focus on worst-case scenarios at school, in sport or at home. Catastrophising can present in different ways, either by focusing on a current situation and magnifying it out of proportion, or by worrying intensely about future possibilities that haven't happened yet and might not occur at all.

Having negative thoughts from time to time is normal, as is thinking about

> **"THOSE WHO STRUGGLE WITH THEIR MENTAL HEALTH ARE MORE SUSCEPTIBLE"**

possible outcomes of a situation, both good and bad. Catastrophising goes beyond this into the irrational. Most people will experience catastrophising at some point, but it becomes a problem when it happens a lot or is impacting on day-to-day life. Signs of this can include racing thoughts, feeling overwhelmed, being unable to move on from the thoughts in your head, negative self-talk, overthinking, focusing intensely on a situation, and constantly looking for an answer online or through seeking reassurance from others. Some are more likely to experience catastrophising than others, for example those with low self-esteem, underlying mental health conditions, fatigue, being a perfectionist or suffering chronic pain (see the box to the right).

Coping strategies

If catastrophising is having a huge impact, then professional intervention is usually needed to help retrain the brain to handle negative thoughts and reframe your way of thinking. Therapies such as CBT (cognitive behavioural therapy) and MBCT (mindfulness-based cognitive therapy) can help you to learn how to identify, control and reframe negative thought patterns.

However, there are also things you can do to help with catastrophising if you notice that this is something you're experiencing more often. For example, getting to grips with mindfulness can help; rooting yourself into the present moment can help to lift the focus off worrying about the future. This could be achieved through meditative practices revolving around perspective and gratitude, or by journalling your thoughts to help recognise patterns and triggers.

Some people find that catastrophising and worrying can take over their day, so it can be helpful to put into place a specific time slot to worry. Give yourself that space to think about all those 'what ifs' that are playing on your mind, but set a strict limit and when that is up, it's time to move on. Worrying is natural, but catastrophising comes from focusing only on negative outcomes and feeling out of control. Instead, it's better to focus on problem solving and finding solutions, which can help you to feel more in control again and therefore your worries are less likely to snowball.

Underpinning all of this is a need for self-care, looking after your own basic needs, such as sleep, exercise, fresh air, water and a healthy diet – when we're in a good physical and mental state, we're far more likely to be able to manage stressful situations in a balanced way, without heading into a negative spiral.

CATASTROPHISING AND CHRONIC PAIN

One area that has been more widely researched is the role of catastrophising in those who suffer from chronic pain, often called 'pain catastrophising'. This is when those who experience regular pain exaggerate the outcome of this pain in their mind or have negative thought patterns towards their actual or perceived pain, limiting what they're able to do or what they can cope with. For example, someone who has a chronic back problem might catastrophise the pain to the point that they feel unable to do exercise, even if exercise has been prescribed to help with the underlying cause of the pain, making the problem worse and increasing pain levels further. Numerous studies have shown a link between pain catastrophising and worsening chronic pain outcomes, including one that highlighted pain catastrophising as an independent predictor of chronic pain following knee surgery[1]; and another that concluded those with irritable bowel syndrome (IBS) reported worse psychosocial and functional outcomes if they catastrophised[2]. While positive thinking won't get rid of chronic pain, managing negative thought patterns can help with the perception of pain, as well as helping to boost motivation for pain management strategies.

[1] Burns L et al. Pain catastrophizing as a risk factor for chronic pain after total knee arthroplasty: a systematic review. *J Pain Res.* 2015
[2] Sherwin LB et al. The association of catastrophizing with quality-of-life outcomes in patients with irritable bowel syndrome. *Qual Life Res.* 2017

GRADES OF *Grief*

Whether you're struggling with losing someone close to you or coming to terms with the death of someone who wasn't, grieving is a very personal process

WORDS SARA NIVEN

Freud once wrote that grieving was a natural process that should not be tampered with.

In reality, dealing with losing someone dear to us is one of life's hardest challenges. The process we go through is different for everyone, and sometimes help can be necessary as we try to navigate it.

Grief can also be complicated. Perhaps the person we've lost wasn't as dear to us as we would have ideally liked (if at all) and we're confused as to how we should feel or react. Alternatively, we may be mourning a pet we regarded as a family member but others can't fully comprehend our devastation.

"The process of grief is unique and how we express it also varies culturally; some people will be left feeling they are not grieving properly or meeting societal expectations of how they should be doing this," says psychologist Ingrid Collins, the director of the Soul Therapy Centre in London. "But there is no right or wrong way, it is a very personal thing. This is even more the case if a bereavement has added complications. Suffering the loss of someone from a dementia-related condition for instance, involves a grieving process while the person is physically alive. This can be more harrowing than mourning an actual death, as the grief is experienced in conjunction with the feeling of being in limbo."

Stages of grief

The five stages of grief were first identified in the book *On Death and Dying* by Elisabeth Kübler-Ross in 1969. She categorised grief into five distinct stages: denial, anger, bargaining, depression and acceptance. Although these sound as though they naturally run consecutively, it is not uncommon to skip stages, get stuck in one or go back and forth between them. The relationship you had with the person you've lost and the circumstances of their death can also influence how you progress through them.

Denial

This is a first line of defence against overwhelming emotions. People will say or think things along the lines of, 'This isn't happening/they will walk through the door any minute/the doctors must be wrong'.

When someone dies suddenly and tragically, denial is very understandable – it is hard to come to terms with a person being absolutely fine one minute and not here the next. However, it is a common reaction regardless. People have talked about calling a recently deceased person's phone for example, even though they are aware they cannot answer. During this period, you may still be in a state of shock and not feeling much at all besides disbelief and numbness.

Anger

As reality emerges, so too can anger. This can be directed at anyone, including the person who has died. If we felt angry with them while they were alive, the emotion can feel particularly overwhelming.

"Anger can be a reaction to the fact somebody can no longer interact or share their feelings with the deceased person," explains counsellor Pauline Couch who runs the Step4ward Counselling Support and Training agency in Dorset, UK. "That can compound any sense of that experienced when the person was alive, leading to feelings of guilt and missed opportunities to sort the relationship out. It can also turn inwards so the person is angry at themselves as well as the deceased."

Bargaining
We replay events repeatedly in our head, wishing certain situations or circumstances could be changed – that if 'such and such' hadn't been the case, the death could have been prevented or delayed. If your relationship was not ideal, you may also berate yourself for not reaching out to resolve issues before it was too late.

"This is incredibly common – I regularly hear people talk about if only they had done this, that or the other," says Collins. "From a young age, we believe we are omnipotent, and as we grow some of that leaves us but there is often still a lingering sense that we should be able to control things, even the circumstances and timings of a death, which very clearly we can't."

Depression
Although depression is generally seen as something that is helpful to be diagnosed and treated, after a death, overwhelming feelings of sadness, not wanting to get out of bed or not feeling up to the demands of daily life, are a natural stage in the grieving process.

With the right support and the passing of time, we start to function normally again. How long this takes varies. Complicated grief – when someone is still experiencing these difficulties many months, even years later, whereby they have lost all motivation and/or even wish they had died too – is another issue and worth seeking medical help for.

Acceptance
The final stage of the grieving process represents coming to terms with our loss. This doesn't mean we won't still feel sad or have bad days, rather that we recognise someone is not coming back and our emotions start to stabilise as we adjust to a new reality without them. »

> "YOU MAY BERATE YOURSELF FOR NOT RESOLVING ISSUES"

Some stages of the grieving process will be more relevant to certain situations than others. There may be very little of the denial or bargaining stage for the relative of someone elderly who dies peacefully after a long and happy life, and is now considered 'at peace'. Conversely, those close to someone who dies young or very tragically could spend a long time in both, and struggle for years to reach acceptance. Sometimes anger over a senseless death or a strong desire to change what happened can be harnessed into a driving force by relatives who campaign for a change in law or seek to hold someone accountable for their loss.

The stages are not a blueprint, more a pathway that can be stepped off, walked backwards at times or deviated from. We are also individuals, dealing with different situations and circumstances in our own way; some people show a lot of outward emotion as they grieve, others very little.

No regrets
Grieving when there are things left unsaid or done can be additionally difficult. "Regret is the lousiest thing to be adding to grief," confirms Collins. "Depending on their views, some people may seek relief in these kinds of circumstances by visiting a professional medium, others can find help in the form of therapy. When clients have unresolved issues with someone who has died or a longing they'd done or said something, it is important to try to process this to move forwards."

A 'no send' letter is an exercise sometimes suggested by counsellors. This can include anything you wanted to say and couldn't express or didn't get the chance to, be it anger, betrayal, hurt or love. This can be a very effective tool in enabling people to move on.

One client in therapy reports writing a letter to a deceased parent they felt upset with, explaining why. They initially intended to put the envelope in the coffin but after writing it, their anger lifted and instead they were able to put their feelings to rest at the same time as their parent.

Another option is what therapists refer to as the 'Empty Chair'. For those comfortable with role playing, it involves speaking to a chair as though the person you want to address is sitting in it. In some circumstances, you may consider swapping chairs and replying from the other person's perspective.

Delayed grief
Sometimes we experience grief a long time after a person's death but that doesn't mean we don't face the same pain as if they'd just died yesterday. This can be hard for others to understand, and they may not show the

HELP IS ON HAND

If you are struggling with loss, or dealing with any aspect of unresolved grief and need support, in addition to one-to-one counselling there are other support systems available to you:

* Cruse Bereavement Care and Cruse Bereavement Care Scotland (www.cruse.org.uk) is the UK's largest bereavement charity and provides free counselling. You will find details on its website of places to contact for help in specific circumstances, such as grieving for someone with dementia or after a suicide.

*Winston's Wish (www.winstonswish.org) offers support for children, young people and their families in the UK after the death of a parent, sibling or significant carer. Parents can access free professional advice for supporting a grieving child.

*Pet owners in the UK can contact the Pet Bereavement Support Service run by the Blue Cross (8.30am to 8.30pm) on 0800 096 6606, www.bluecross.org.uk/pet-bereavement-and-pet-loss.

*Griefline (https://griefline.org.au) is a free helpline in Australia that provides nationwide telephone support (1300 845 745) from 8am to 8pm seven days a week.

> "GRIEVING WHEN THERE ARE THINGS LEFT UNSAID OR DONE CAN BE ADDITIONALLY DIFFICULT"

same empathy as they would for someone experiencing a recent bereavement.

"I had a very dear friend I hadn't seen for decades due to circumstances and many years later found out they had taken their own life," recalls Collins. "They were someone in the public eye and I later ended up reading a book about them – it wasn't until then that my grief fully hit me."

If you haven't seen someone for many years, finding out they have died can be a shock. If they represent a specific time in your life that has now passed, you may find yourself mourning part of yourself in addition to the person. Their death can also highlight the upset of any past fallouts or separation the two of you had.

Grieving for a pet

"Losing a pet can be as devastating as losing a relative or close friend for a pet owner, as there is often a very strong bond there and pets are part of, or sometimes a person's only, family," says Diane James, Pet Bereavement Support Service manager at national pet charity Blue Cross.

"It's important that people take the time to grieve a pet, as with any loss, and we fully support understanding employers who offer bereavement leave to allow time for pet owners to come to terms with their loss. Every year we are contacted by more than 12,000 owners who have been left devastated and struggling to cope after losing a pet."

As counsellor Pauline Couch, points out, animals can often play a vital role in some people's lives as a source of comfort, in addition to companionship.

"Some people have animals to support them emotionally around issues such as anxiety, low mood, low self-esteem or debilitating illnesses," Couch explains. "Once that pet dies, it can leave the person feeling unsupported and very alone. I have had many clients who have lost family members and coped with those well, but when their pet died it felt even bigger, because their support was no longer there to help them through the grief and pain."

Losing an estranged relative

One in five UK families are affected by estrangement according to UK charity Stand Alone, while a US study reported that 10% of mothers had no contact with at least one adult child.

Not having any contact with a parent might appear to make their death easier to come to terms with but it doesn't necessarily work that way. We have still lost part of our heritage and will likely mourn any possibility of an apology or reconciliation. There will also be the pain and loss experienced by other family members we do have a close relationship with to factor in.

Even if you were not estranged, a complicated relationship with a parent can still be highlighted when they die. Jayne Harris lost her father a year ago and says grieving alongside her siblings was a difficult process. "My dad had seven children by two marriages and his relationship with each of us was different. One son refused to come to the funeral, while another was so upset at my father's death, he struggled to go back to work. On a personal level, I found my dad tricky to deal with; he'd say hurtful things sometimes and could be very critical.

"Even so, I underestimated the impact of his death. In the funeral home I wanted to hug his body, even though I had sometimes held back from that when he'd been alive. It brought up a lot of childhood issues and in talking about his life with others who'd known him, I gained a better understanding of why he was the way he was and wished there were things we'd discussed. My brothers and sisters were all affected so differently, and my experience of him as a father didn't quite fit anyone else's.

"Since his death, I've experienced anger, guilt, regret and a deep sense of loss, both for the father I had and the one I'd ideally wanted. It took his death to know there was love between us. Ironically, I feel it more now than when he was alive."

When you really didn't like someone

It may not be a good idea to shout it from the rooftops at their funeral but the simple fact is that not everyone deserves to be mourned by you to the same extent as a loved one – if indeed they deserve it at all. If someone maliciously made your life a misery, abused or generally mistreated you or was simply not a very nice person, there is nothing wrong with you or the need for guilt if their death just leaves you feeling relieved or indifferent.

Not speaking ill of the dead does not need to mean speaking good of them if you genuinely have nothing positive to say. If others feel differently, then it is just about respecting that and a personal decision as to if you attend the funeral. If you do, out of respect for other people (if not the deceased), the best course of action is either to keep quiet or say something neutral but truthful, such as being sorry for their loss or it being hard to find the right words.

PAWS FOR THOUGHT

Danielle Tanner is a veterinary nurse in the UK. She lost her beloved Labrador, Taz, and says it is hard for some people to understand the bereavement felt by pet owners.

"Taz was my best friend and went everywhere with me from the moment I got him as a rescue dog. My friends, family and co-workers who knew what he meant to me were fantastic and when I cried at work, I had sympathy and understanding. The pain is still very real and I am lucky to work in a profession where people know first-hand how much an animal can mean.

"However, nobody expects you to need any time off work as they would a human relative. Colleagues gave me allowances such as not having to speak to the public that day or dealing with any 'put to sleeps' for a while. But others who were not animal people expected me to act like nothing had happened. Some assumed I'd immediately replace him or felt I'd be okay because I have two other dogs."

Danielle says she had enough support but if that hadn't been the case, she would have called the Pet Bereavement Support Service run by the Blue Cross.

"People need to know there are places to turn and it's a helpline I'd like to be part of. Something that helped me was to have some of Taz's ashes made into a ring. The company who did it treated it with as much respect as if he were human, which meant a lot."

OVERCOMING IMPOSTOR SYNDROME

It's a self-inflicted feeling that holds you back, burns you out and saps your motivation – and it's time to get it sorted

WORDS TRISHA LEWIS

There it goes again: that nagging, negative feeling that you are barely getting away with it. Any minute now, they will find out that you are a fraud! You may have done a good job, but that was by fluke more than skill. You might have fooled them into giving you this promotion, but within weeks you will mess up and the truth will be out. It is obvious that you will never be the real deal – not like those grown-up people over there.

But what if your brain is tricking you into believing your feelings represent reality? Do these impostor syndrome feelings stand up to scrutiny?

What is impostor syndrome?
You might have heard the phrase 'impostor syndrome' before, but what does it really mean? The term first appeared in 1978, in a research article by Doctors Pauline Clance and Suzanne Imes. While the original phrase given to this set of feelings was 'impostor phenomenon', the term 'impostor syndrome' became more widely used. The problem with the word 'syndrome' is that it suggests a medical condition, when in this case it is no such thing. It is a feeling that can come and go. It is a brain trick – a 'cognitive distortion'. Doctor Clance said that in hindsight she would have used the term 'impostor experience'.

Terminology aside, what is impostor syndrome? How is it relevant to you? And what can you do about it? The first point to emphasise is that this is about feelings, not an infection or broken bone. We are talking about a self-inflicted feeling. If you are doing it to yourself, it must surely be easy to fix, right? Achievable, of course, but not easy.

With knowledge and practice, you can get a grip on the negative effects of these feelings – but never underestimate the power of emotions.

What does impostor syndrome feel like?
To overcome it, you need to be able to recognise it. It's a disconnected sensation – as if you are on the outside looking in.

TRISHA LEWIS
COMMUNICATION COACH

Trisha Lewis is a UK-based professional communicator with a special interest in impostor syndrome, hosting workshops and building communities. As an actor, speaker and communication coach, she is passionate about spotting and sorting everything that blocks confidence and connection.

WWW.TRISHALEWIS.COM

The others have a right to be there, but you don't. It is the gnawing feeling that if you take your eye off the ball – if you stop doing your utmost to be loved, accepted and perfect – then you will be ostracised by a jeering crowd of haters who have discovered the useless or unlikeable you. It is a feeling of embarrassment when people praise you –

OVERCOMING IMPOSTOR SYNDROME

they are just gullible or polite. It is a feeling of surviving rather than thriving. You are not alone in having these feelings.

Jodie Foster describe it like this: "When I won the Oscar, I thought it was a fluke [...] I thought everybody would find out, and they'd take it back. They'd come to my house, knocking on the door: 'Excuse me, we meant to give that to someone else. That was going to Meryl Streep'." However, it might not have been accepted by Meryl Streep. She too experiences impostor syndrome feelings, which she describes like this: "You think, 'Why would anyone want to see me again in a movie? And I don't know how to act anyway, so why am I doing this?'"

But surely it doesn't affect the likes of all-round superwoman Michelle Obama, or acclaimed *Love Actually* screenwriter Richard Curtis? Yep, them too! Even Albert Einstein described the feeling when he said: "...the exaggerated esteem in which my »

" "

lifework is held makes me very ill at ease. I feel compelled to think of myself as an involuntary swindler." You see, even the best of us experience this. It is a human condition.

Away from the world of the famous, let's look at some everyday feelings that you might recognise:

I feel 'weak' when I ask for help

I feel I need to be perfect, or the game's up

I feel that I must show proof of my capabilities

I feel like I can't be the real me

I feel that my achievements are more fluke than skill

I feel awkward when given compliments

I feel reluctant to take on new challenges in case I fail

I feel weary from 'faking it'

I feel as though others in my group [business/friends] are better than me

I feel anxious when not in control

I feel strangely 'alien' a lot of the time – as if looking in from the outside

Do any of these feelings resonate?

What if the feelings are left unchecked?
Some feelings lead you astray, like hearing a car backfire and fearing for your life; or seeing a stranger in a café who reminds you of someone bad, and feeling anger towards them. They are very real feelings followed by responses that make no rational sense. While

> "EVEN THE BEST OF US EXPERIENCE IT. IMPOSTOR SYNDROME IS A HUMAN CONDITION"

COGNITIVE DISTORTION

Impostor syndrome feelings are your brain distorting reality. The father of CBT (cognitive behavioural therapy), Aaron T Beck, coined the term 'cognitive distortion' to describe the inaccurate version of reality and irrational thought patterns that can lead to states of anxiety and depression. Here are some of these 'distortions' that are relevant to the feelings of impostor syndrome.

DISQUALIFYING THE POSITIVE
Giving little thought or value to positive events. Underestimating your value to others. Assuming your success is more of a fluke than a deserved outcome. Feeling awkward when given compliments.

EMOTIONAL REASONING
Giving precedence to emotional negative feelings rather than rational reality. You feel it, so it must be true.

MENTAL FILTERING
Only allowing the negative to get through your filter, and making sure your brain confirms your already present negative beliefs. You always look stupid when you voice an opinion, so that look they just gave you was confirmation of how stupid you are.

JUMPING TO CONCLUSIONS
Going straight to the negative, without passing scrutiny. Acting like a mind-reader and fortune-teller.

MAGNIFICATION AND MINIMISATION
Your failure is huge; your success is tiny. The threat is massive; the opportunity is minimal. You got four out of five on that one item on the feedback form – this is the one you obsess over.

So what's the best way to get back to reality?
The pause and reframe tactics that are at the heart of CBT are highly effective tactics to sort your impostor syndrome feelings.

OVERCOMING IMPOSTOR SYNDROME

> "YOU NEED TO PRESS PAUSE AND GET RATIONAL WITH YOUR EMOTIONS"

gut instinct can provide a healthy decision filter, blindly responding to every feeling with an action or decision can lead to negative consequences. We're going to look at some of these – this should motivate you to work on reframing some of your impostor-syndrome-fed responses. Let's group the consequences into three categories:

Hide-out

Burn-out

Freak-out

This probably needs some explanation.

Why 'hide-out'? Think about it: when you are constantly doubting yourself and living in fear of being 'found out', it follows that you might keep your head down, try to blend in, agree rather than express your perspective, or even walk away from new opportunities. You are unlikely to voice your achievements and things you should be proud of – you mistakenly believe that this would come across as arrogant. Worse still, they would think: 'Wow, they are so full of themselves, and goodness knows why!'

Why 'burn-out'? You're trying too hard to please and be perfect. Perfectionism is a big symptom of impostor syndrome. There is nothing wrong with doing a good job, but if you impose ridiculous standards on yourself for fear of falling short and being found out as a fraud, well, you will burn out.

Why 'freak-out'? You become a living pressure cooker, and bottling up all those suppressed emotions is not good for you. That urge to break free and show the world a less filtered version of you... all that effort you make to be accommodating for the sake of being accepted... all that inexplicable fear teetering on the edge of anger... In the pressure cooker of impostor syndrome, these feelings have no way of escaping – until something goes wrong and the whole thing explodes! If you never let off steam, you risk exploding at the wrong time and place, with dire consequences. You erupt in anger during a meeting, you slam a door so hard that it breaks, you hand in your notice in a dramatic outburst... you get the picture. In an ideal world, you want to avoid all these negative consequences. It's time to get your impostor syndrome under control.

Is there a cure?
Unfortunately, there is no quick fix for impostor syndrome. There is no cure because it is not an illness or broken bone as we established earlier. It is a feeling. You can't stop feelings, and you shouldn't attempt to. We feel – we are human. Many of our negative thoughts are there to protect us. We have the same brain wiring as our ancestors did back in our hunter-gatherer days. We need a healthy dose of self-doubt to prevent us regularly running into danger. However, impostor syndrome is not this kind of natural, healthy self-doubt – it is not helpful. It is a trick, an illusion – it is your own brain giving you fake news!

But how do you avoid the negative consequences of impostor syndrome? You need to acknowledge these feelings. Pay attention to them and be aware of how you respond to them. Instead of making knee-jerk decisions that are fuelled by an irrational feeling, use the pause button. It is such a relief when you discover you are in control of the pause button. You own it. The sequence is:

feeling – pause – action

Simple, but so effective.

Your action plan
There is slightly more to it than pressing the pause button, of course. What do you do during this pause? You need to get rational with your emotions. Practise using the pause button, and it will eventually become second nature and empowering. By combining emotion with rationality, you'll find you have far more energy to drive creative thought and complete projects.

Here is how this works in practice: take the feeling and put it through the rationality filter. For example:

Feeling: I feel like a useless child in a world of grown-up professionals.
Rationality filter: Am I a child? Is everything about children useless? Who defines the word 'professional'?

Now ask yourself this: how helpful is this feeling? Only then should you proceed with the appropriate action or decision.

In summary:

1. Press pause between feeling and action

2. Put the feeling through the rationality filter

3. Act on or dismiss accordingly

Although it might feel like a slog to begin with, consciously following this sequence will become a helpful habit.

Here are some other habits to cultivate:

Ask for feedback (even when your brain is telling you to run away)

Keep a daily or weekly 'big myself up' journal

Allow the unguarded 'you' out to play

Talk to others about these impostor syndrome feelings – you are not alone

Knowledge is power when it comes to impostor syndrome – know it, make friends with it and become the boss of it. Give it a name, perhaps even draw your impostor syndrome character. Taking a step back from the nagging, negative chatter inside your head is a good feeling – a relief and a release.

MANAGE YOUR MIND

MANAGE YOUR MIND

Feeling INFERIOR

We explore what it means to have an inferiority complex and how you can overcome it to improve your mental health and wellbeing

WORDS JULIE BASSETT

Feelings of inferiority happen to all of us; we might feel 'lesser' than someone else, whether that's due to their rank, status or ability. It's human nature to compare ourselves to others and we might perceive that, sometimes, we come up short. This can make us feel inadequate, sad or frustrated, but most of the time these feelings pass as we put them into perspective. However, sometimes it's harder to move on from this feeling of 'not being good enough', so much so that it starts to impact on our mental wellbeing, which is when it can become a problem.

Inferiority complex is when a person has sustained and persistent feelings of inadequacy and inferiority, beyond a normal, healthy reaction. So, for example, you might interview for a job and not get it – it's quite normal to feel disappointed and upset for a period of time. However, for someone with an inferiority complex, the level of disappointment and self-doubt felt is usually disproportionate to the event that caused it. Inferiority complex can be experienced due to real, tangible reasons (like a particular physical attribute, or scoring lower on a test than someone else), or it can be due to things that we imagine are true, even if this isn't reflected in real life.

People with an inferiority complex can react in many different ways, from withdrawing from situations that make them feel inadequate, to being intensely competitive to try and compensate for their perceived shortcomings. However, there are some common signs that may help to identify an inferiority complex. A person who feels persistently inferior may be low in self-esteem and often doubt their ability to do something for fear of being compared to others and being seen as 'less able'. They may also be prone to overanalysing situations and conversations; even if comments are positive, they may not believe that they are true. They may also withdraw from social situations in which they feel inferior. Reactions can also »

> **"THE LEVEL OF DISAPPOINTMENT AND SELF-DOUBT IS USUALLY DISPROPORTIONATE TO THE EVENT THAT CAUSED IT"**

LINKS TO OTHER DISORDERS

Inferiority complex, as we've explained, isn't its own diagnosable disorder, however it is often noticed alongside other mental health conditions and diagnoses. For example, feeling constantly inferior can contribute to depression and anxiety, as well as some personality disorders. Feelings of inferiority around the physical body can also contribute to eating disorders or body dysmorphic disorder. It's important to seek the right help and support if feelings of inferiority are present alongside other symptoms that may be commonly associated with these mental health conditions. The first stop is usually your doctor, who may refer you to counselling or therapy sessions alongside other treatments.

---

range from actively seeking out praise and compliments to help validate self-worth, or speaking negatively about others to try to make themselves feel better. Other common signs include negative self-talk, feeling resentful of others, procrastination because of the fear of starting something and doing badly, and perfectionism to try to overcome perceived inadequacies.

Inferiority complex, however, is not a disorder that can be diagnosed on its own; it is a state of mind in which you find yourself focusing on your real or imagined shortcomings more than usual. That's not to say that the treatments for other diagnosed mental health conditions can't be successful in the treatment of an inferiority complex, particularly talking therapies, such as cognitive behavioural therapy (CBT), which can help to reframe your thoughts. There is also a lot that you can do for yourself if you think you have an inferiority complex. If you find yourself fixating on other people and what they have that you don't, or constantly comparing yourself to others to the point it takes over your thoughts, then this can be a sign that you might need a little help.

Impact on mental health and wellbeing

Constantly living in a state where you feel inferior and that everyone is doing better than you can, understandably, have a big impact on your mental health and wellbeing.

This can contribute to certain mental health conditions, like depression or anxiety. Feeling inferior can lead to self-doubt, worry, stress and sadness. Living with these thoughts and feelings over a sustained period of time can make you become withdrawn and not want to engage with your normal social circles or environments. It might also lead to feelings of 'what's the point in trying?'. All of these can develop into a more serious mental health disorder.

You may also find that spending so much time focusing on your perceived inadequacies means that you don't have a good quality of life. You may find that you shy away from social events, or stop doing things you enjoy because you feel like you're not good enough. The problem is that the more you withdraw from something, the less chance you have to improve. For example, feeling inferior at work can stop you from taking on more challenging roles and projects, which may mean that you're passed over for a promotion, which then enhances and confirms your perceived sense of inferiority, making it much more difficult to break the cycle.

The knock-on effect can be that you don't look after yourself as well as you should, which can mean that you don't get enough sleep, exercise or quality food, all of which can contribute to poorer mental health and physical wellbeing.

For some, the impact of living with an inferiority complex can be even more harmful. If you're feeling constantly inadequate and have low self-esteem, you might be more likely to turn to self-destructive habits. This might be drinking more than usual, using recreational drugs, or overeating on low-nutrition 'junk' foods.

When an inferiority complex can develop

There are lots of reasons why normal, occasional feelings of inadequacy can develop into a complex series of relentless thoughts. It usually develops over time, and there are many events or life experiences that can contribute to the development of an inferiority complex. One 2022 study[1] analysed social media posts that indicated inferiority feelings (based on the theory that people often use social media as a way to express their thoughts, even when they might not do it face to face in real life) and found that the common themes behind those feelings were: 'experience, physical defect, personality, love/relationships, ability and social interaction', among others.

For some, it's bedded in the physical; the way that we feel about our own bodies. This can be things like specific disabilities or physical impediments, which can sometimes lead to feelings of inadequacy if we struggle to do the same things as those around us. Or we may struggle with our body shape, height or facial features – we may become overly self-conscious as a result of the way

> "YOU MAY SHY AWAY FROM SOCIAL EVENTS, OR STOP DOING THINGS YOU ENJOY BECAUSE YOU FEEL LIKE YOU'RE NOT GOOD ENOUGH"

we see ourselves and this can make us feel inferior around others. This is often exacerbated by the use of social media, where the ability to compare lives with people from all walks of life, and from all around the world, is at our fingertips.

Feelings of inadequacy can have their roots in childhood and have stayed with us ever since. This could be due to a difficult upbringing, being constantly belittled or put down. Some children are pushed to pursue certain sports, or excel academically, which can lead to frustration, anger and doubt when it's difficult to meet those high standards. It can be hard to shake off this sense of failure as we move into adulthood.

An inferiority complex can still develop after the most secure of upbringings. Sometimes it can be triggered by a specific traumatic event - a serious illness, accident or loss of a loved one, for example. It can also develop because of life challenges, which could be financial (not earning as highly as peers, for example), social (feeling like our lives are not as exciting as others') or professional (we're not as high up the career ladder as we 'should' be).

Family dynamics can be difficult and may sometimes contribute to feelings of inadequacy. This can be true if, for example, a sibling is particularly high achieving or if there is a sense of favouritism from parents. This can lay the ground for comparison and competition from a young age. Even as an adult, we might struggle with having to justify our life choices to parents or feel like we've let them down if we don't follow a specific path. Personal relationships and friendships in adulthood can also be triggers, however we have more choice in these connections, often being drawn to people who are similar to ourselves and therefore we may be less likely to engage in regular comparison or competition.

Coping with an inferiority complex
If your life is consumed by thoughts of inadequacy, it can be very difficult and challenging. It takes a change in mindset, from a state of mind in which you feel inferior, to a place of acceptance - i.e. learning to be at peace with the person you are right now, no matter what's going on around you. This means learning how to catch those negative thoughts when you sense them, and reframe them in a more positive way. You can acknowledge the thought and consider its truth. Is it a fact? Has something concrete happened to cause the sense of inferiority? What can you learn from that? Or is it something that you perceive to be true, but has no basis in reality? How can you control that?

INFERIORITY AS A MOTIVATOR

We all experience a sense of inferiority from time to time; it's a normal part of life to compare ourselves to others. When these feelings of inferiority and inadequacy take over our thoughts and negatively impact on our daily lives, that's when it becomes an issue. However, sometimes a small dose of inferiority can be a positive thing. For example, when we see a highly trained athlete compete, we might feel inferior to them, but it could still motivate us to want to go out and do that sport. At work, we might see a colleague doing great things on a project and feel inferior, which could then incentivise us to take steps to improve ourselves and our career. A little sense of feeling inferior can, from time to time, be a good thing, driving us to push ourselves, as long as our mental health and happiness don't rely on it.

Keeping a journal can help, giving you somewhere to unspool your thoughts and make sense of them. Often the act of noticing and acknowledging your thoughts can be the first step towards acceptance. Try to also use the space to think of positive affirmations you can incorporate into your life - remind yourself daily of your strengths and positive attributes, to counteract the negative feelings of inadequacy.

You don't have to do it alone. You may wish to speak to a professional, particularly if it's affecting your everyday life. However, even talking with friends and family can be a big step. They can help to put things into perspective, give you a reality check and remind you of what you're good at.

There is only one 'you', so relish your uniqueness and individuality. We can't all be amazing at everything, so there will always be those who are better than us throughout our life in certain areas. But life's not a competition and no one should make us feel like we're inferior, not even ourselves.

DEVELOP A *positive* BODY IMAGE

How do you feel about your body? Transformational coach Alison Morgan uncovers the power of gaining a fresh perspective of yourself

DEVELOP A POSITIVE BODY IMAGE

WORDS ALISON MORGAN

Our bodies are truly amazing. Carrying us, keeping us alive, creating new life, healing wounds... the list goes on. But these are all things we tend to take for granted and, as amazing as we are, we often struggle to see ourselves in a positive light.

In a social-media-frenzied world, often showing the 'perfect' life or body, having a positive image about our own bodies seems to be increasingly challenging. In one click, it's easy to be thrown into a scenario of comparing ourselves with others and wishing we had the perfect legs, bum or lips (take your pick!), and if we're not careful, it can lead to a downward spiral of self-loathing, low confidence and a negative body image, which can impact all areas of our lives.

As much as we know it's healthy and important for us to have a positive view of our own body, many of us struggle with this daily act of self-acceptance and compassion. So how would life be different if we liked or even loved our bodies a little bit more, and how can we achieve this?

What does a 'positive body image' really mean?

We all see things in different ways, and the concept of a 'positive body image' is no different. It's about how you perceive yourself. Think of it as:

How you see your body

How you feel about your body

The thoughts you have about your body

The things you do that result from this self-perception

Think about how you perceive yourself on a scale of 0-10, rather than simply seeing yourself either positively or negatively. This will probably change on a weekly, daily and even hourly basis due to things happening around you, but the more you start to become aware of how you're feeling about yourself, the better placed you are to take action to move the scale towards confidence, more of the time. Think baby steps more frequently, rather than giant leaps less often.

This isn't about seeing yourself as perfect – perfect doesn't exist. It's also not a destination that you get to and stay at. It's an ongoing work in progress, much like physical fitness; it's something that needs regular attention to make lasting differences and for you to feel more comfortable in your own skin.

To love or to loathe?

We only get one body to carry us through our lives. It's the only thing that you will spend your whole life with, and you have a choice: look after it, nourish it and learn to love it, or waste precious time and energy loathing it, beating yourself up and comparing yourself to others. You wouldn't say negative things to your friends, so why say them to yourself?

True, long-lasting, deep confidence and a healthy perception of your body comes from within. It comes from you accepting yourself, treating yourself kindly, working on being a healthier you, and having positive opinions and beliefs about yourself. It's always lovely to receive compliments from people, but you can't live off these forever. They should be nice to have, not necessary to have.

Living with a negative body image can drain us, control us, and steal our happiness and enthusiasm for living life.

Improving your attitude towards yourself may just turn up your happiness dial. It might not be an easy journey, but wonderful things will happen if you give it a go! What have you got to lose?

A more positive mindset

Being more positive about ourselves more of the time sounds simple, but in reality it can

> "MANY OF US STRUGGLE WITH THIS DAILY ACT OF SELF-ACCEPTANCE"

take some work and commitment. Here are some simple areas to start thinking about:

Develop a healthy attitude towards yourself
Developing a healthy, positive attitude towards yourself as a whole, complete human being may mean a shift in mindset, but it is achievable. Nothing positive comes from a negative mindset, and the sooner you start practising this through making small shifts, the sooner you will feel the benefits. Everything is in your power to change; you simply need to believe in yourself.

Explore your thoughts and feelings about your body
Learning to shake off negative beliefs and opinions about yourself may help you move »

WRITE DOWN ALL THE THINGS YOU LOVE ABOUT YOUR BODY

DEVELOP A POSITIVE BODY IMAGE

towards a place of acceptance and respect for your body. Learning to tune in to the thoughts that chatter away in our heads, and learning to have the courage to face the negative ones rather than avoid them, is an important stage in the healing process.

Take action that works for you
On your journey to becoming more positive about your body image, you'll find the things that work best for you. Face the challenge with a learning mindset and be comfortable with taking action and trying new things. Stick with them and build up your toolkit, so when you feel your confidence slipping, you know what tool to pull out!

Put it into action
How often have you thought: 'When I lose this weight, I'll be more confident and happy'? Yes, you might be, but often the effect is short-lived. You're then looking for the next thing and the next. The trick is to start working on your body confidence now, and that starts with your mindset and becoming healthier and stronger physically and mentally at the same time.

Ready to get started? Begin with these simple actions…

Develop a healthy attitude towards yourself:

Accept yourself as the unique individual you are today. Don't let your mind wander back to the past or dream about the future. Practising mindfulness will help train your brain to be more focused on the present and reduce this time travel of your mind.

Focus on your own journey, rather than wasting time comparing yourself to others. You will never be them.

> **" IT MAY REQUIRE A BIT OF TIME, TRIAL AND ERROR TO FIND WHAT WORKS FOR YOU, BUT IT'S WORTH IT "**

Don't be mean, critical or judgemental to anyone – including yourself! Be kind, supportive and show compassion.

Work to improve yourself, but don't strive for perfection. Enjoy the journey you're on, learning what works for you, and be proud of every small achievement you make towards a healthier, stronger, more positive version of you.

Respect yourself and all that your body has taken you through so far in life. Write down three things you're grateful to your body for each day.

Put yourself first – develop a great relationship with yourself. If you don't, it's harder to have effective relationships with others.

Be so proud of yourself; you don't need compliments to make yourself feel better.

Explore your thoughts and feelings about your body:

Be curious about how you honestly feel about yourself, and try to go beyond 'I don't like my body'. Try closing your eyes and slowly focusing on each part of your body and see what thoughts, feelings and emotions arise.

Dig deep and try to understand why you feel that way. Can you link it back to something that happened in your past?

Develop the ability to tune in to the thoughts that regularly chatter away in your mind. Try keeping a journal to capture how you feel about your body daily. Notice any themes and things that trigger you to feel worse or better.

Notice when your mind wanders through the day to thoughts about your body. When you notice this has happened, try to focus back on the present moment, whatever you are doing, or your breathing.

We often avoid thoughts that are uncomfortable or painful. Instead, learn to observe them and how they make you feel. This isn't about solving them, but exploring them might bring new insight and reduce their power.

Take action that works for you:
It may require a bit of time, trial and error to find what works for you, but it's worth it. Building a personal toolkit of exercises to use when your thoughts are slipping to the negative will keep you on track to having a positive body image.

The long-term change will come from the internal work you do, but there's also fun stuff, like wearing great clothes that flatter you, treating yourself to a facial, or just spending time with loved ones. Have fun with it all and remember that true beauty is much more than skin deep.

YOU CAN FACE YOUR *Fears*

We're told to feel the fear and do it anyway, but that's sometimes easier said than done. Rather than dreading something, we take a look at finding ways to embrace the fear

WORDS DEBRA WATERS

If you're someone who is distrustful – superstitious, even – of change, these feelings can infiltrate decisions you make, big and small. BIG: it might take ten years of careful consideration, spreadsheets and sleepless nights to move to a different city. SMALL: your daily habits are so set in stone that you bore yourself (same morning coffee, same jogging route, same lunch at the same café). But do you try something new? Nope. And if, for some reason, you have to alter your routine, does your anxiety go into overdrive? Why have you become so change-averse?

One explanation is 'better the devil you know'. Fear thrives on uncertain outcomes. For instance, you work on an uncomfortable chair that hurts your back – changing it might make your back worse, although it could make it better. More concerning are unhealthy relationships people hold on to, so as not to cause upset or a fuss, or experiences they reject in case they disrupt their carefully curated life. Sometimes, even though we become more comfortable and settled, rather than using this stability as a springboard to a more stimulating life we become more fearful than ever. Yet change can be inspiring and insightful. It enables us to adapt, learn and evolve, and it keeps boredom at bay. So why do many of us find it daunting?

Fear is physical
"Our responses to change are not always conscious or even within our control," says »

YOU CAN FACE YOUR FEARS

SIGNS YOU NEED TO FACE YOUR FEAR

You...

- let opportunities or experiences pass you by

- avoid spontaneity, yet crave it

- feel unchallenged, bored or stuck in a rut

- envy others who seem to live more fulfilling lives

Becky Hall, a life coach and author of *The Art of Enough* (£14.99, PB, Practical Inspiration Publishing). "Our brains and nervous systems are hard-wired for predictability. Neuroscience shows us that the oldest part of our brain creates patterns quickly – we like to be able to predict what will happen next. So, when unexpected things happen, or we're not certain about how things are going to turn out, our brain responds as if we're in danger. This triggers our nervous systems into high alert, which is why we get anxious."

Could this mean that those of us prone to anxiety are more susceptible to fearing change? The way we react to excitement is sometimes barely distinguishable from a bad case of the nerves. For worriers, our default tends to be fretting over things that could go wrong rather than things that could go right. Perhaps we should give exposure therapy a go, starting with minor, manageable changes to increase our confidence.

Facing your fear

Fear of change isn't always negative. Caution can be self-protective, a gut instinct even. Sometimes it's a reaction to what's occurring in the world, such as the cost of living, which has made many of us fearful of changes to our financial stability. "The key is not to get overwhelmed," says Becky. "We want to be proactive not reactive, so taking time to calm our nervous system, breathe and think positively is crucial. Then we can look at choices we have to make calmly."

But what if we're faced with the unavoidable, such as redundancy? "One trick is to think about something or someone in your life that's certain or predictable," suggests Becky. This is reassuring and provides an anchor.

It can also help to draw two circles, one inside the other, says Becky. "In the inner circle, write down things that you can control or influence; in the outer circle write down things you can't do anything about. Focus on what you have written in the inner circle – things you can do something about. This puts you in your full agency and gives you real choices about things that you are able to affect."

Ultimately, to fear change is to fear loss – of a loved one, our livelihood, wellbeing or security. But playing it safe doesn't shelter us from possible losses – if anything, being too rigid can work against us. American writer Elbert Hubbard wrote, 'The greatest mistake you can make in life is continually fearing that you'll make one'. With this in mind, let's consider the pros and cons of the next change we need to make, and make an informed, panic-free decision. When we look at it rationally, we have nothing to fear but fear itself.

Stop fear from stopping you

"Finding something we can do to improve our health and wellbeing – even a small action – puts us back in the driving seat, and that alone makes us feel better," says health coach Lou Walker (louwalker.com). Here are some expert suggestions...

CALM YOUR MIND
There are real and useful ways of calming our nervous systems down, and reassuring them that we are

> "THINK ABOUT SOMETHING OR SOMEONE IN YOUR LIFE THAT'S CERTAIN OR PREDICTABLE. THIS REASSURES AND PROVIDES AN ANCHOR"

YOU CAN FACE YOUR FEARS

not in danger, says Becky, who suggests two easy ways to self-soothe. First, slow your breathing and think of something positive, she says. "Counting to four as you inhale then exhale calms our nervous system and helps us reset in the present moment. Secondly, go to your happy place. Thinking of something that makes us smile creates 'happy' hormones that override the hormones triggered by stress," says Becky. "When you feel physically calmer you will feel less afraid to make decisions."

TACKLE RELATIONSHIP PROBLEMS
Often, we fear asking ourselves questions that need answering, but once you've said yes or no you're in a stronger position to move on. Do you want to end your relationship? Yes. Then do it, says counsellor Margaret Ward-Martin (thegraceproject.co.uk). Do you want to end your relationship? Yes, but I'm scared. Then do it scared. "There's no avoiding the pain," says Margaret, "but if you circumvent discomfort it will likely come out in unhealthy ways, so embrace the process."

STOP SELF-MEDICATING
Fear can be hard to live with, so we may self-medicate to numb the nagging anxiety that we need to take action. But we can't face fear if we're using avoidance tactics. It could be a little something to take the edge off the fear – work, wine, prescription medication, illegal drugs, risky sex – but only by accepting the situation can you mitigate some of this fear, says Margaret. Give yourself a chance to tackle changes with a clear head, rather than self-anaesthetising.

IMPROVE YOUR DIET
Is fearfulness connected to the food we consume? Well, we are what we eat. "Our diet affects brain health, mood and thinking," says Lou. "Start by cutting out sugar and ultra-processed foods. This is tough, but start small – it helps. Improving diet lifts mood, clears brain fog and improves depression." If you feel brighter, you're more likely to feel confident about making changes.

ADDRESS YOUR FINANCES
By confronting monetary concerns you can make constructive changes. "Identify what's keeping you up at night," says financial expert Makala Green (makalagreen.com). "Pinpointing the source of your stress will provide clarity. Then create a budget – identifying where your money is going can help you save money for areas causing financial concern." If it's too overwhelming, consider using a financial planner – in the long-term you could save more than this costs.

THINK LIKE A SUCCESSFUL PERSON
If your fear of change is motivated by a fear of failure, try changing your mindset. "Successful people fail!" says Lou. "If you don't try to change something, it might mean you don't fail, but if you don't try, you definitely won't succeed. Trying and failing gives you the chance to learn why it didn't work that time so you can tweak your approach before trying again."

TRUST THAT YOU'LL BE OKAY
If you're fearful of something but you own it, you – not what's worrying you – are in control. Keep busy with healthy things that occupy you. "Being distracted can be restorative," says Margaret. And be kind to yourself. "Change requires effort and sometimes you won't feel like it – that's okay," says Margaret. "A duvet day is in order sometimes, but not if you become depressed (if this is the case, please see your doctor for support). You will be fearful – and you will also be fine."

WHERE DOES IT ORIGINATE?

Fear feels like a purely emotional response, but it has a physical origin. "When the amygdala – the part of our brain that controls our fight/flight/freeze response – gets triggered, the energy in our brain is focused on danger. That's great if we're at risk but unhelpful if it happens when we're about to do something that requires our best thinking," says Becky. "Emotions come into it because our amygdala sits on top of the hippocampus, which stores memories," she continues. "This means that, sometimes, a fight/flight/freeze response reminds us of a time when we were worried, or something went wrong. So, not only are we reacting as if we're in danger in the present, but we're connecting it emotionally to past events or trauma. This can lead to anxiety and worry, emotional withdrawal or even actively protesting about things changing at all."

THE ART OF Letting Go

Learning to 'move on' might seem impossible at first, but it can leave you happier and healthier

WORDS SAMANTHA WOOD

Ever feel like you just can't come to terms with something that has happened? It's time to stop beating yourself up. The inability to 'get over it' or 'move on' is down to our biological and evolutionary make-up, so if you're finding something hard to accept, it's very much not your fault.

The act of accepting, closing the door and moving on from things – whether that's an unattainable goal, the dissolution of a relationship or the loss of a loved one – is extremely challenging as it's almost like admitting defeat, says body psychotherapist Jessica Eve (kaylolife.com). "We naturally fight against it because our bodies have learned that they need to fight to survive. However, being in a state of non-acceptance can leave us feeling stuck or trapped. Plus, if steps aren't consciously taken to move on after an adverse experience, the body often won't allow the experience to be forgotten, which can lead to the depletion of our mental and physical wellbeing."

Here's why – and how – we should take steps to accept...»

> " BEING IN A STATE OF NON-ACCEPTANCE CAN LEAVE US FEELING STUCK OR TRAPPED "

THE ART OF LETTING GO

THE ART OF LETTING GO

Trapped by the past
Feel you get stuck in a wallowing rut after a break up? When things go wrong, or we experience emotional pain and trauma, our brains like to hold on to the details, poring over the information and re-running the tape, to try and make sense of what happened and to prevent it from happening again. Traumatic experiences can also foster a wish to be able to go back in time and have things play out differently, which is why we often find ourselves obsessing over them, wishing things had been different.

"Our brains are determined to work it out and learn from the experience, preparing us for if and when the situation reoccurs," says Hannah Bailey, a psychotherapist in BWRT – Brain Working Recursive Therapy (bluelightwellbeing.uk). "If the nervous system is not soothed and down-regulated after an adverse experience, the body does not trust that learning from the experience has taken place and won't allow it to be forgotten – keeping us stuck in that uncomfortable moment."

> **TRY TO CONNECT WITH YOUR FEELINGS AND BE HONEST WITH YOURSELF ABOUT THEM**

The inability to move past something and reliving past traumas over and over uses up a lot of energy and can have a massive impact on not just our mental and emotional health, but our physical health too.

"I very rarely see anyone without health problems caused by the things they can't move on from," continues Hannah. "Headaches, joint pain, insomnia and irritable bowel syndrome (IBS) are just a few of the ways that trauma, post traumatic stress disorder (PTSD) and bereavement can manifest themselves in our bodies, which is why it's so important to work towards acceptance."

Getting back to the present
Learning how to accept something can also lower stress levels, improve our relationships and aid concentration.

Acceptance is so beneficial because it is one of the most liberating states of being, says Jessica. "We are usually much more present and in tune with our physical bodies, helping us to release stress and tension we might otherwise not know we're holding. This reduces levels of stress chemicals such as histamine and cortisol, which are responsible for lots of inflammation – too much of which is linked to illness." Jessica adds that we also become more responsive and less reactive, fostering more flexibility of mind to better solve problems, be more creative and improve our relationships.

It also allows us to be more connected with the wider world. When we are in a high state of tension and our suffering is ongoing through non-acceptance, we lose a lot of our capacity to truly engage with our environment.

"Cultivating acceptance therefore positively influences our capacity to experience pro-social and pro-environmental impulses," says Jessica. "For example, if you are stuck in anger you are far more likely to drive recklessly and behave in a way that just doesn't serve you."

You don't have to forgive to forget
Moving on from something where you've been left feeling hurt or wronged – maybe a betrayal, a broken friendship or a divorce – doesn't have to involve you giving someone your forgiveness. So if that's the thing holding you back, don't let it. "In many situations, the thought of forgiving someone to be able to move forward can be impossible, creating immediate resistance," says Hannah, who specialises in working with families who have been bereaved by murder or manslaughter. "I encourage my clients to change the word 'forgiveness' to something else that might be more achievable for them – for example, feeling more 'peaceful' or even just being 'indifferent' to the person and the trauma. In doing this, you move towards softening the feelings and toxicity surrounding the situation and with time it should have less power over you."

Don't fool yourself
Be wary of mistaking other things for acceptance. "Defeat, denial or suppression can often masquerade as acceptance," warns Jessica. "Sometimes, people so desperately want to be in a state of acceptance that they completely deny their true feelings – even to themselves."

So, what does acceptance feel like? Obviously, it can feel different to everyone and according to Jessica, "in a state of acceptance, it is perfectly normal to feel grief and joy," so try to connect with your feelings and be honest with yourself about them. "Acceptance is also often spoken about as if it's a simple choice you can make: 'just' accept what it is," she adds. "Remove this pressure from yourself. Sustained acceptance is a state of being that takes time, support and slow cultivation. Fortunately, the blueprint for acceptance already exists within us."

Soothe your nervous system
Establishing a daily practice that soothes the nervous system will help in taking steps towards acceptance. Things you can do at home are chanting or singing (especially with other people), breath work, meditation and using gentle therapeutic touch, such as 'havening'.

6 STEPS TO A HEALTHIER MIND & BODY

Learn to adapt and move on with these expert tips

1. ACKNOWLEDGE IT
The first step in being able to accept something is to respect, honour and acknowledge it. "If it's difficult to move on from, that usually shows that it had some kind of importance or significance in our lives, even when it's something we'd never have wished for," says psychotherapist Eloise Skinner (eloiseskinner.com). "Once we acknowledge that it deserves time, space and attention, we're much more likely to be able to begin properly processing it."

2. HOLD A RITUAL
It might sound a bit 'woo-woo' but Eloise says that holding a symbolic 'letting go' ritual can help with closure and moving forward, in a similar way that funerals help us acknowledge and accept the loss of loved ones. "It could involve throwing out old items or memory triggers, refreshing your personal space with spring cleaning, or reorganising or writing a letter and then burning or burying it," she suggests. "You may also choose to involve honouring the loss, reminding yourself of any lessons learned or things to be grateful for, and setting goals for the future."

3. TRY THERAPY
Our brains like repetition and will often go for familiar thought patterns, so therapy techniques like Brain Working Recursive Therapy (a short-term therapy designed to permanently change the way your brain reacts to certain stressors) can be hugely helpful in creating new neural pathways – a vital part of acceptance and moving forward. "It's a very successful technique and people generally only need about six sessions," says Hannah.

4. FIND AN OUTLET
Finding a way to channel your emotions or reflect on the thing you're moving on from – like a creative hobby or chatting with friends – can be very cathartic. Daily journalling is an affordable, easy and effective option, perhaps using a prompt like 'what do I need to let go of today?' "Having an outlet for your thoughts and feelings might then make it easier to look ahead at what's coming next and how you can reform your own sense of identity in line with what you consider to be important for your future," says Eloise.

5. CONNECT WITH NATURE
It sounds simple, but switching off your phone and going for a walk, run or wild swim outdoors, is the best way to get positive energy moving through the body, putting us more in touch with our genuine feelings. "Connecting with nature widens our perspective, gives us a stronger sense of being held by the world, and of having our own place in the wider matrix of life," says Jessica.

6. BE MORE MINDFUL
Practise mindfulness during daily activities. "If we allow ourselves to become present, our breathing changes and our bodies relax: we are not stuck in the past or worried about the future," says Jessica. Catch yourself if you are thinking or talking about the thing you want to accept and move on from and ask yourself: Do I feel more or less energised? What's happening to my breathing? Can I feel my feet on the ground? Simply drawing attention to the body in the present moment can be hugely helpful.

Bad Habits AND HOW TO BREAK THEM

Discover some of the most common repetitive behaviours that can lead you astray and how to best break the cycle

WORDS SCOTT DUTFIELD

What exactly is a 'bad' habit? We often associate the term with classic examples such as biting the ends of your nails, eating fast food or smoking. While these can indeed be undesirable behaviours, the scope of what can be classed as a bad habit is vast. Defined merely as any repetitive behaviour that has a negative or detrimental effect on your life or health, bad habits can manifest in a myriad of ways. From fighting the urge to go to sleep just so you can see what's happening on social media to heading to the beach without first putting on sun protection, sometimes it's the bad habits we are unaware of that can cause the most damage. However, there are many simple ways to fight bad habits, even if you've had them for many years. Ultimately, understanding the underlying problems that trigger them may be key to breaking them.

NAIL BITING

Gnawing at the ends of your nails, for a lot of people, manifests in moments of anxiety, stress or simply as a bad habit. As many as 30% of the population bite their nails, with teenagers being the biggest perpetrators. It may seem like a harmless habit, except for leaving your nail a little jagged, but by continually chewing your nails, dirt and bacteria are being transferred into your mouth, putting you at greater risk of infections. Nailing biting is a habit that often develops as a child, so tackling it at an early age can help prevent the long-term effects.

In the past, preventing nail biting involved coating fingertips with bitter- or sour-tasting foods. However, today there are many nail-polish products that have the same effect. Creating a physical barrier between the mouth and nail, such as gloves, mittens or even a mouthguard, can also help to break the habit. Maintaining short nails is also a method to alleviate the problem, preventing the habit from being able to manifest.

For the more severe cases, known as onychophagia, nail biting may have a connection to your mental health, such as anxiety or depression. In these cases, cognitive behavioural therapies can be explored to understand the emotional root of the habit, and seek to remedy the underlying problems.

USING SPECIAL BITTER-TASTING VARNISH TO TACKLE NAIL BITING CAN HELP PEOPLE GET OVER THIS BAD HABIT.

EATING TOO QUICKLY

Sitting in front of a freshly delivered pizza or a gooey chocolate brownie, it's easy to get lost in the excitement of the flavour explosion that's about to follow. However, for some people, it's an experience that's over in a matter of moments. Not only bad dinner-party etiquette, eating too quickly can be a bad habit that affects your health. Studies have shown that those who are quick to munch on a mouth-watering meal have a greater risk of obesity and developing metabolic syndrome, a group of conditions including heart disease and diabetes, when compared to those who take their time to chow down.

To remedy rapid eating, the solution can be quite simple: slow down and savour the flavour of your food. It's believed that it takes around 20 minutes for the stomach to signal to the brain that it's full. Therefore, to make sure you're giving your body enough time to catch up, spend at least 20 minutes on each of your meals. This isn't to say you have to spend this amount of time continually eating at your usual speed, but rather increasing the time spent on your usual portion size. »

> **"COGNITIVE BEHAVIOURAL THERAPIES CAN BE EXPLORED TO UNDERSTAND THE EMOTIONAL ROOT OF THE HABIT, AND SEEK TO REMEDY THE UNDERLYING PROBLEM"**

BAD HABITS AND HOW TO BREAK THEM

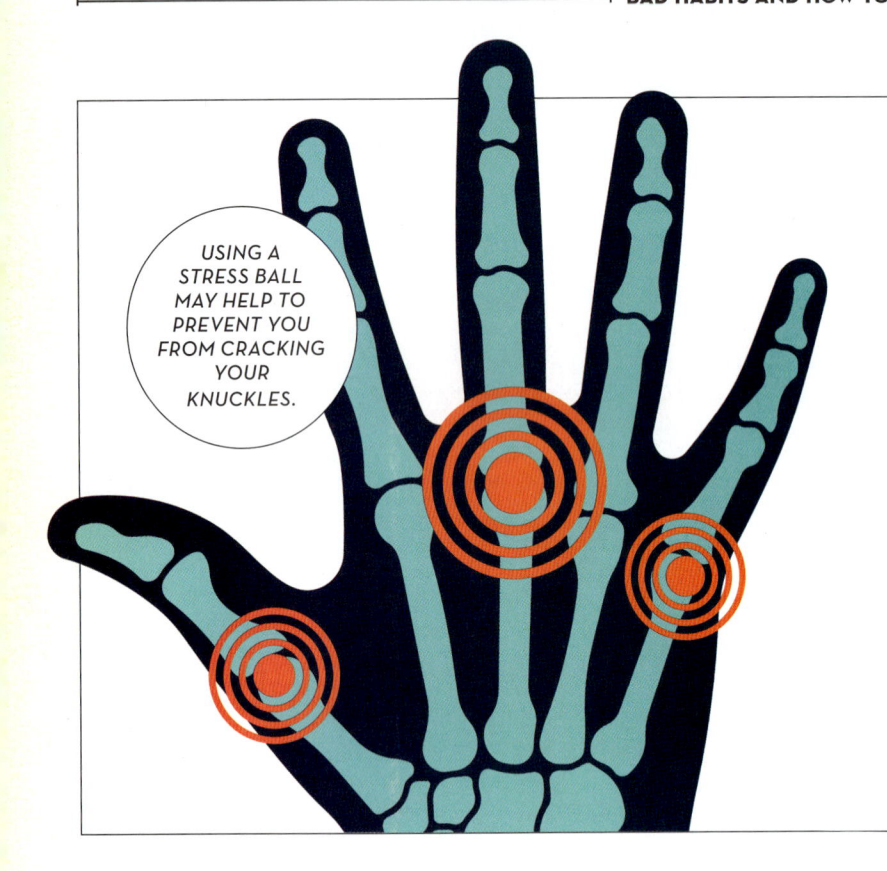

CRACKING KNUCKLES

There is still a debate on whether cracking your knuckles can be classed as a bad habit due to research suggesting no connection between doing so and the development of arthritis, as previously believed. However, there are still concerns over potential injuries that can occur while self-cracking. Overall, jerking your knuckles back and forth to release the build-up of gas bubbles between your finger joints may lead to the weakening of your grip or even promote swelling.

Occupying your hands may offer some relief against the compulsion to crack, for example squeezing a stress ball. It has also been suggested that putting an elastic band around your wrist, pulling it back and releasing it to snap against your skin when you feel the need to crack may create a negative association with the consumption and train you to stop. This method can also be used with a range of bad habits, such as nail biting.

USING A STRESS BALL MAY HELP TO PREVENT YOU FROM CRACKING YOUR KNUCKLES.

SUCKING YOUR THUMB

It's a naturally occurring instinct to suck your thumb as a child, typically dissipating as a habit after the age of five. However, many adults carry the behaviour into later life. It's believed thumb sucking may release an endorphin rush, similar to that which occurs when infants breastfeed. Although it may provide a sense of comfort and relaxation to engage in this habit, it can cause problems in later life. Often leading to the misalignment of your teeth or affecting the roof of your mouth, tackling this habit can be similar to that of nail biting. Covering your thumb with a glove or coating it in a bitter taste may help to wean you away from this bad habit.

AROUND ONE IN TEN ADULTS STILL SUCK THEIR THUMB.

PICKING SCABS

There can be something satisfying about finding a scab and picking it straight off, especially when you're a child. However, there is a good reason why your parents scolded you for doing it. When the skin is cut or scraped, a scab develops to act as a protective barrier over the repairing skin beneath. By removing this layer you increase the risk of infection and the time it will take to heal. To break this bad habit, distraction may be key. By preoccupying yourself with another task such as reading, drawing or grabbing a fidget spinner you can offer relief from the compulsion to pick.

— BAD HABITS AND HOW TO BREAK THEM —

> "ONE OF THE REASONS SMOKING IS SO DIFFICULT TO GIVE UP IS THE EXPERIENCE OF DAILY TRIGGERS THAT MAKE YOU WANT THE TEMPORARY RELIEF A CIGARETTE MAY PROVIDE"

USING A PHONE IN BED

We can all be guilty of scrolling through social media while tucked up in bed. However, staring at your smartphone before sleep can be a bad habit. The blue light emitted from your phone has been found to suppress the production of night-time hormone melatonin. As part of our body's natural 24-hour cycle, the setting of the sun signals that the time to sleep is near, and so our bodies produce melatonin to relax the muscles and dull the nervous system to ease us into a deep slumber. However, the light emitted from our phone hijacks that signal and delays melatonin production, resulting in a disturbed sleep cycle. This can lead to tiredness and insomnia.

To prevent this bad habit from disturbing a good night's sleep, allow for one hour between updating your online profile and hitting the hay. Of course, smartphones aren't the only perpetrator for interrupted sleep: tablets and TVs can have the same effect. If the temptation to log on is too much, leave your device in another room and use a digital alarm clock to keep your schedule. »

AROUND 1.1 BILLION PEOPLE IN THE WORLD SMOKE ACCORDING THE WORLD HEALTH ORGANIZATION.

SMOKING

Arguably one of the worst routines to develop, smoking can lead to a host of problems. A nicotine-fuelled addiction, smoking is more than a bad habit – it's been linked to several health concerns including cancer, heart disease and respiratory conditions.

Unlike solving some bad habits, there isn't one single way to quit smoking. Tackling both addiction to nicotine and the behavioural practice of lighting a cigarette can be difficult. That being said, many alternative products, such as patches and gums, have been proven to satisfy the need for nicotine without ingesting the harmful chemicals within a cigarette.

One of the reasons smoking is so difficult to give up is the experience of daily triggers that make you want the temporary relief a cigarette may provide. These triggers can include stress, anxiety, boredom and socialising with other smokers. Addressing the root of the triggers may also alleviate the craving to smoke.

USING YOUR PHONE BEFORE BED CAN LEAVE YOU FEELING TIRED THE NEXT MORNING.

MANAGE YOUR MIND

BAD HABITS AND HOW TO BREAK THEM

SLOUCHING AT YOUR DESK

In a world where everyone is sitting in front of a computer or smartphone for the majority of the day, it's easy to find yourself hunched over a keyboard. Poor posture can lead to back pain, circulation issues and fatigue.

To get you on the straight and narrow while seated at your work desk, sit so your knees are parallel with your hips, and raise your computer screen to your eye line with a straight back. Making sure you have a chair with a supportive backrest will also help to prevent you slouching forward. While you are hunched over, tension builds between your back muscles and causes discomfort. Taking time to get up and walk around will relieve some of that tension.

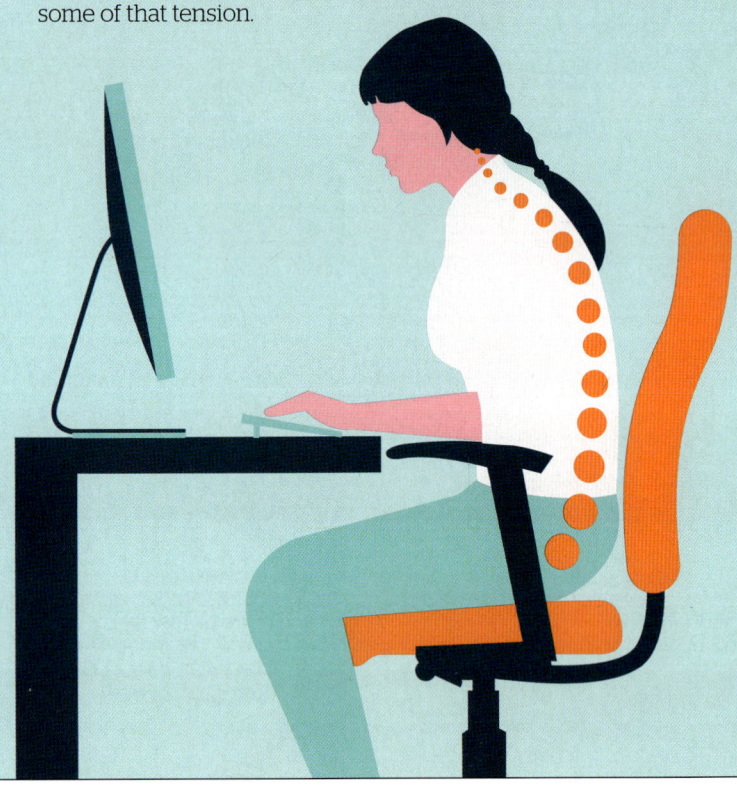

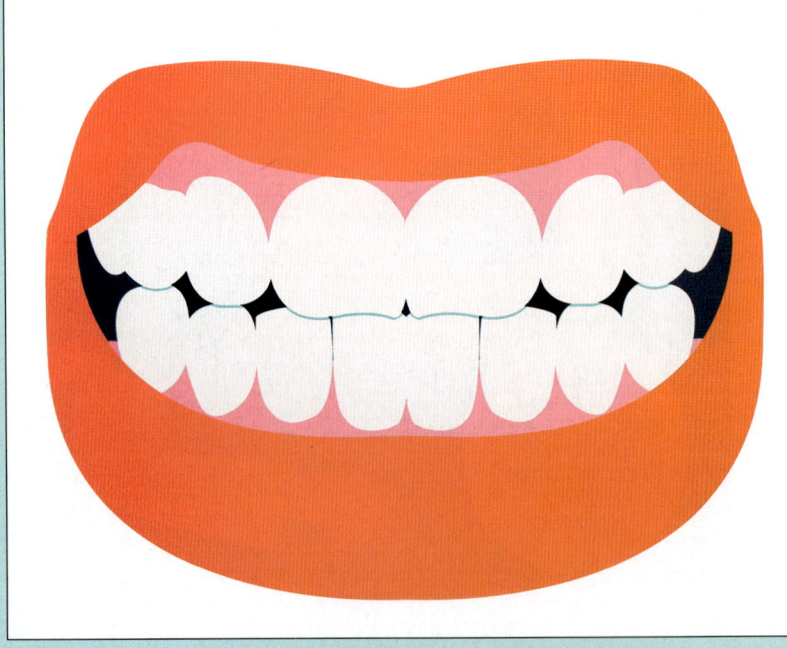

MONEY WORRIES HAVE BEEN LINKED WITH SEVERAL SERIOUS HEALTH CONCERNS, WITH OVERSPENDING BEING A LARGE CULPRIT.

OVERSPENDING

Financial stress can have serious health consequences, from high blood pressure to depression, so spending outside your means when you should be budgeting can have a bigger effect on your life than a low bank balance. Overspending is a bad habit that can be a tricky one to confront because the only way to overcome it is with self-discipline. Creating and sticking with a budget can help keep you in the black. In extreme cases, overspending can lead to racking up large amounts of debt. By freezing your credit cards, you may be able to nip the problem in the bud before it gets out of control.

GRINDING YOUR TEETH

In moments of stress and anxiety, many people have adopted the habit of tightly clamping their jaws together and grinding their teeth. Aside from wearing down your teeth, this bad habit can lead to headaches, jaw stiffness and even earache. In many cases, the person exhibiting this behaviour isn't even aware they are doing it. Often occurring during sleep, night grinders wake up with jaw pain and no recollection as to why.

To tackle teeth grinding, first addressing the root of the problem may be the solution. Meditation, therapy and exercise for the release of endorphins may help to keep your stress and anxiety levels in check and in turn keep your teeth from coming to blows. However, for the unconscious sufferers, using a mouthguard while you sleep will help to prevent the damaging effects of teeth grinding.

MANAGE YOUR MIND

BAD HABITS AND HOW TO BREAK THEM

EATING FAST FOOD

The temptation to grab a juicy cheeseburger or a greasy bucket of chicken can be hard to fight. And while having a cheeky fast food meal every once in a while isn't necessarily a 'bad habit', when a server at your favourite burger joint knows your order off by heart, it's probably time for a change. It's no surprise that fast food can have negative effects on health when eaten regularly. From heart disease to obesity and diabetes, eating food filled with high levels of fat and sugar can wreak havoc on your body.

A good way to help ditch a fast-food habit is to make sure you don't reach the point of feeling overly hungry. When ravenous, junk food presents itself as a quick fix, meaning we are less likely to take the time to make a home-cooked meal. By creating a weekly plan, you can stay on top of your hunger and out of a greasy spoon.

> **"TO PREVENT PUTTING TASKS OFF UNTIL THE LAST MINUTE, SET YOURSELF A DAILY SCHEDULE, LISTING SIX OR SO OF THE MOST IMPORTANT THINGS YOU NEED TO ACHIEVE THAT DAY"**

PROCRASTINATION

Whether it's washing the dishes, answering a work email or writing that school essay that's due tomorrow, procrastination is a bad habit that can affect many different aspects of your life. Other than the stress and anxiety caused by rushing to finish a task you've put off completing, procrastination can lead to you challenging your self-worth, producing poor-quality or incorrect work, and fatigue.

To prevent putting tasks off until the last minute, set yourself a daily schedule, listing six or so of the most important things you need to achieve that day. Also, be realistic in what you can achieve in your given time frame. Overreaching your goal or underestimating how long a task will take might leave you challenging your abilities, furthering your desire to put them off in the future. It also doesn't hurt to try out a reward system for each task. By only doing your favourite things once you've carried out a task, you might be more likely to achieve your goals. You can also do some of these simultaneously: play your favourite TV show while you're doing household chores like ironing, or eat your favourite snack only while you do school work. »

DON'T LEAVE IT TO THE LAST MINUTE – BEING PROACTIVE WITH A TASK WILL HELP YOU IN THE LONG RUN.

MANAGE YOUR MIND

WASTING FOOD

It's difficult enough to break a bad habit when you're aware of it, but trying to change a habit that you didn't know you had can be seriously challenging. In a world where sustainability is a hot topic, how we dispose of food waste could reveal an unknown bad habit.

It often comes naturally to simply throw food into the household waste bin without giving it a second thought. In the UK alone, around seven million tons of food are wasted each year. However, by purchasing a garden composter for organic material, you can drastically reduce the amount of waste you send to landfill, and your garden will benefit from a nutritious fertiliser.

For those foodstuffs that are approaching their best before date, many community apps such as Olio connect local people to exchange and give away food rather than disposing of it.

AROUND 1.3 BILLION TONS OF FOOD MADE FOR HUMAN CONSUMPTION IS WASTED OR LOST GLOBALLY EVERY SINGLE YEAR.

SKIPPING BREAKFAST

It might not seem like a bad habit to ditch the morning toast and head straight to work, but repeatedly ignoring a critical meal of the day can be a routine with negative consequences. There's a reason why they call it the most important meal of the day, and that's because it kick-starts your metabolism. Leaving it until later in the day to chow down has been linked to health concerns such as weight gain and blood-sugar fluctuations. To keep your metabolism in check, make sure you grab a bite bright and early.

INTERRUPTING

Life is full of uncontrollable interruptions, whether it's an unexpected flat tyre or a nonsense marketing phone call. But there is something particularly annoying about being interrupted during a conversation. Cutting someone off mid-sentence is something many people have been guilty of doing, but being a repeat offender can be socially detrimental, particularly in the workplace. Verbal interruptions can suggest that you regard what you have to say as more important than what someone else is saying. In the workplace, this behaviour may change; for example, people are less likely to stop their boss mid-sentence.

If you are guilty of this, try to take a second before you speak and let the other person finish. If what's on the tip of your tongue is a critical comment to the conversation and you're worried you might forget it, simply jot it down on a notepad and wait for the right moment to speak without cutting anyone off.

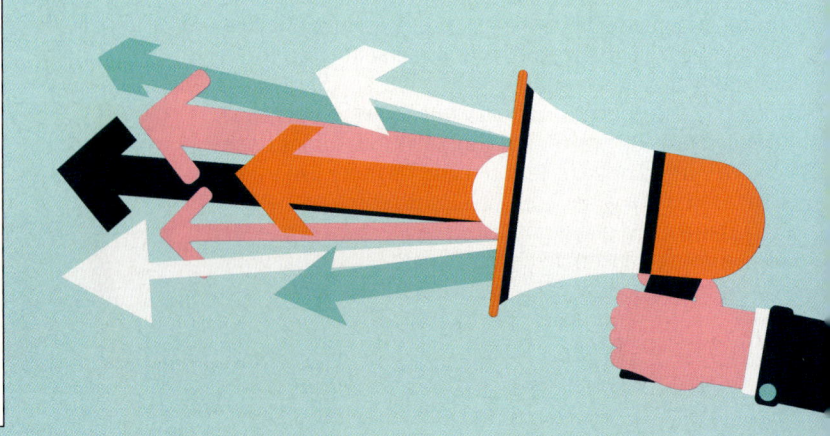

NOT USING SUNSCREEN

If you love to bask in the sunlight during the summer months but neglect to apply sunscreen in the hope of developing a golden tan, you may be unwittingly exposing your skin to a whole host of future problems. Exposing unprotected skin to ultraviolet (UV) radiation can increase the risk of developing skin cancer and promotes premature ageing. While sunbathing, UV rays weaken the fibres in the skin that keep it smooth and youthful, leaving skin wrinkled and leathery. The same can be said of visiting sunbed salons. The UV radiation from a tanning booth produces the same radiation found in the sun, presenting the same risks.

To beat the burn and stay safe during the summer, always carrying a travel-sized sunscreen in your bag is a great way to make sure you have protection against the Sun with you at all times. You can also harness the power of modern technology, which has taken away most of the guesswork when it comes to keeping an eye on the sun. Downloading apps such as UVLens can notify you when the UV levels in your area are high and when to apply sunscreen to avoid getting a burn.

A SUN TAN OR BURN IS THE BODY'S WAY OF DEFENDING ITSELF FROM HARMFUL RADIATION.

HAVE THE BEST OF BOTH WORLDS AND TAKE THE EXERCISE BIKE WITH YOU WHEN YOU WATCH TV.

BEING A COUCH POTATO

Slumping across the sofa in front of the TV after a long day at work or on a lazy Sunday afternoon might be considered by some as the perfect 'me time' – the ideal way to chill out and unwind. Perhaps for an hour or two a day that might be true, but what about for five hours or even an entire day? Getting into the bad habit of spending extended periods being sedentary increases the risk of depression and obesity, and can even affect your personality, making you less agreeable and conscientious.

Keeping an active routine and rigid TV schedule is the best way to prevent becoming a couch potato. It's recommended that you only spend around two hours per day sitting watching TV, and at least 30 minutes exercising. Channel surfing or binge-watching the latest Netflix show can be hard to resist, so only tune in to watch a specific show and try to limit how many episodes you watch in a day. If you just have to see how the series ends, take the treadmill or exercise bike from the spare room, put it in the living room and exercise while you watch.

> "ALWAYS CARRYING A TRAVEL-SIZED SUNSCREEN IN YOUR BAG IS A GREAT WAY TO MAKE SURE YOU HAVE PROTECTION AGAINST THE SUN WITH YOU AT ALL TIMES"

Meditation & THE BRAIN

Training the brain to remain in the present moment can ease stress, reduce anxiety and even lower blood pressure. But how does it work?

WORDS LAURA MEARS

The English word 'meditation' comes from the Latin *meditari*, which means to think or to ponder. But the practice has its roots much further east than Rome. It originated in India as early as 4,000 years ago, before spreading eastwards to China and Japan, and westwards along the Silk Roads into Europe. Now, as brain scans begin to pinpoint the neurophysiology of meditative experiences, and research trials explore the effects meditation practices can have on our wellbeing, what began as a step on a spiritual path towards enlightenment is fast gaining a reputation as a panacea.

Neural rewiring for health and wellbeing

There are hundreds of different ways to practice meditation, but at their core, most use a form of focused awareness to calm and balance the mind. Though research is still in its early stages, trials are starting to reveal the difference that even a short meditation practice can make to health problems like depression, anxiety and insomnia.

It's important to note at this stage some of the challenges inherent in unpicking the effects of meditation on the mind. It is notoriously hard to design studies that truly measure subjective effects on mood and wellbeing, and due to the sheer number of different meditation practices, it's often difficult to compare the results from one trial to the next. The meditation experience of study participants can be variable, as can the length and duration of the practices they're asked to perform as part of each trial.

The absolute gold standard in medical research are randomised controlled trials. In these studies, participants are randomly separated into two groups: one receives the experimental treatment, while the other receives a different treatment or placebo as a 'control'. This enables researchers to really measure the difference that the experimental treatment makes. But designing a control for meditation trials is tricky.

When researchers at Johns Hopkins University trawled through more than 18,500 meditation research studies in 2014, they found only 47 that met their strict criteria for proper study design and control. But within those 47 high-quality research papers, there were some clear psychological benefits: an eight-week meditation practice showed to improve symptoms of anxiety, depression, stress and pain.

This pattern of improvement in mental health problems is mirrored elsewhere in the meditation literature. Separate studies have found that meditation helps to boost lifespan, improve quality of life, lift mood and decrease anxiety for people with cancer. It helps to prevent relapse in people experiencing repeated bouts of depression. And, it can help people to cope with the symptoms of menopause and irritable bowel syndrome.

Meditation also has positive effects on wellbeing in people without underlying »

MEDITATION AND THE BRAIN

> **" MEDITATION HELPS TO BOOST LIFESPAN, AND DECREASE ANXIETY "**

MEDITATION AND THE BRAIN

LEARNING TO LET GO

Steve Harrison dedicated his life to the practice and teaching of yoga after a transformational experience with a yoga master. We asked him why learning to meditate is so hard, and what we can do to make it easier.

"I think for me the first thing to understand is that meditation is a state, rather than a practice. It's convenient to say 'I practice meditation', but it's not really the case. We can create an internal environment that is conducive to slip into a meditative state, but you can't actually do meditation because meditation is where doing ceases to happen."

WHY IS IT SO HARD TO LEARN TO GET INTO A MEDITATIVE STATE?

"In a modern world, it can be unrealistic to ask a mind to be able to focus. The obstacle that most people encounter almost straight away is their own bodies. Physical discomfort is, for a lot of people, a distraction from letting go into meditation. Sore knees, sore hips, backache… the body just keeps interfering. Focus techniques are an incredibly subtle device that require an immense amount of willpower. It can turn into a fight with ourselves to try to calm the mind when the body is not agreeing."

WHAT CAN WE DO TO MAKE IT EASIER?

"The ancients spent thousands of years devising ways to help people manoeuvre into a meditative state. It wasn't only the mind that was worked on. If you can do simple things to work with your body and your breathing, it will do a lot of work on the mind without the fight. But the biggest thing for me, and I think the least spoken about, is our own psychology. Most of us are incredibly identified with our thoughts and our sense of individuality. In order to not constantly be pulled back into a thought stream about ourselves, we need to have a genuine interest in finding a space or an experience that's beyond our usual constructs of who we think ourselves to be.

"Ask yourself, how would it be if I just let go of myself for a moment? We don't disappear as a result of slipping into meditation, we expand."

health problems. It seems to improve working memory, focused attention and emotional regulation. In one study, participants listened to either a guided meditation or a language lesson. Then they were challenged with disturbing images. Those who had meditated were much quicker to recover from the emotional hit.

A quiet space and a comfortable seat
So how does meditation change the way our minds work? Many other tools that help us with emotional control usually work on the parts of the brain involved in conscious, rational thought. But meditation practices work differently. Rather than actively trying to control our thinking, meditation techniques train us to draw our attention away from the parts of the brain involved in reasoning and judging, and towards the more ancient structures that are involved in awareness of the present moment.

The brain constantly monitors incoming signals from the outside world, passing them through a structure just above the brainstem called the thalamus. It works like a comms relay, taking in sensory signals and forwarding them on to other parts of the brain for processing. Filtering this stream of information is an active process; we constantly and consciously have to choose what to focus on.

Our focus decisions are complicated by an additional stream of information, the

> **MEDITATION TECHNIQUES DRAW ATTENTION AWAY FROM REASONING AND JUDGING**

sensations from inside our bodies. These are detected by the insula, the part of the brain responsible for interoception, or internal self-awareness. It responds to feelings like pain, hunger and thirst, but also has a role in emotional awareness, and links in with other parts of the brain involved in attention.

Deciding what sensation to focus on falls to a wide circuit of connected brain regions called the 'salience network'. It uses the anterior insula (the internal sensor), the anterior cingulate cortex (the attention allocator) and the amygdala (the fear centre), to listen in on external and internal sensations, before then working out where we should put our focus. And it changes when we meditate.

Meditation practices almost always begin by taking a comfortable seat in a quiet space. This helps to minimise the internal and external sensations fighting for our attention and, over time, starts to change the way the salience network operates.

During meditation, the thalamus remains active, still passing signals into the brain. But, with fewer distractions, the mind has room to focus in on sensations that often go unnoticed, like the feeling of the breath.

In experienced meditators, the connections in the internal-sensing insula change and strengthen, improving internal awareness, and grey matter in the attention-allocating anterior cingulate cortex increases, aiding focus and flexible thinking. Meanwhile, the prefrontal cortex, which makes decisions, weakens its connection to the fear-inducing amygdala. One study found that after just eight weeks of meditation, the amygdala even started to shrink in size.

On a whole-brain scale, imaging studies have discovered even more widespread changes. Measures of white matter thickness show that meditation can boost connections in the front of the brain, which contains areas involved in attention and emotional regulation. Simultaneously, regular meditation practice seems to prune connections towards the back of the brain, in areas that are involved in self-referencing and egocentric processing. »

TRY THIS AT HOME

Yoga teacher Steve Harrison shares a simple four-step meditation practice for beginners. This is an indirect method to do a lot of work on the mind without actually having to fight with the mind. Sit down, get comfortable, take some long, deep breaths, and create an environment inside in which the mind can actually start to focus.

BRING THE BODY INTO A COMFORTABLE SPACE
The one key is to be comfortable. Any form of physical movement or intuitive stretch can make sure that the body is as fluid as possible. Then ensure that the body is in the most conducive state to relax, without falling asleep. Sit on a chair, or in an armchair, but always ensure you have a straight spine in order to keep the brain-body connection alert.

SORT OUT YOUR BREATHING
If you're looking for the quickest way to create an equilibrium in your system, the breathing is the key. The state of the breathing reflects the state of the mind. If the breathing is agitated, the mind is agitated. If the breathing is calm, the mind will also become calm. Just gently start to control and deepen and steady the breathing in order to calm the mind without directly trying to control the mind.

FOCUS ON DEEP BREATHS
It's unrealistic to sit down and try to just watch your natural breath. Don't go too subtle too quickly – you will last seconds and then you'll be off. You'll have this constant ping-pong inside of returning to focus on your breath and then getting pulled back out again. So, deepen your breathing, because deep breathing is much easier to focus upon.

KEEP PRACTICING
You can slip into a meditative state by accident, but to slip into it at will requires lots of training. The mind that's not trained will generally be quite dissipated and unable to hold attention. But it's not necessary for the health benefits and the wellbeing to achieve the meditative state. Commit to regular, patient practice and just reach towards the point of meditation; there are a whole host of benefits that come with the journey.

Cutting out external interruptions and turning inwards during meditation rewires and reshapes the mind.

Focused attention in a wandering mind
Minimising distraction and internalising the mind is just one part of a meditation practice. The other major component is attention training. Many practices have a particular point of focus upon which to fix the attention; the breath, a word or maybe a sensation.

Depending on the focal point, different parts of the brain light up. Mantra meditations activate the auditory cortex. Moving meditations activate the motor cortex and cerebellum. And visual-focus meditations activate the visual cortex. But studies on blood flow in the brain have shown that, rather than direct the attention outside of the body, this kind of activity in a meditative state actually helps us to look inside.

Focusing on a single external sense, like sight, can activate the areas of the brain involved in internal sensing and, while this is happening, a part of the brain called the medial prefrontal cortex slows down.

The medial prefrontal cortex is part of the brain's 'default mode network', the circuits responsible for our sense of self. The network lights up when we daydream, when we think about others, when we ruminate on the past, and when we project into the future. It tends to become active when we withdraw from the world into a resting state, but meditation practice changes how it operates.

Inexperienced meditators often notice that the mind tends to wander during meditation: that's the default mode network activating. It's the brain's way of planning, processing and thinking about itself, and it can run away with us when our senses are internalised. But, with practise, people seem to become better

THE MEDITATING BRAIN

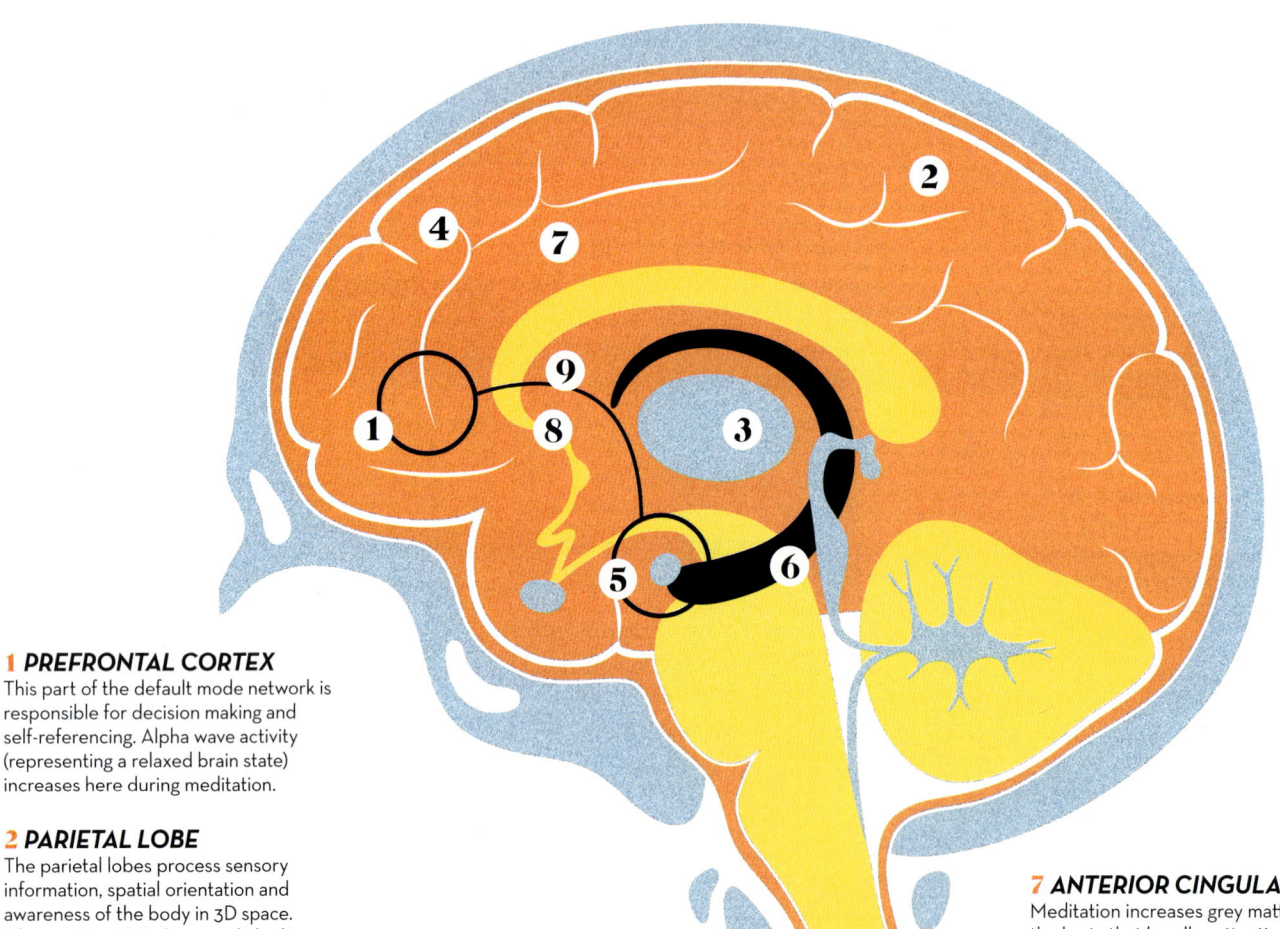

1 PREFRONTAL CORTEX
This part of the default mode network is responsible for decision making and self-referencing. Alpha wave activity (representing a relaxed brain state) increases here during meditation.

2 PARIETAL LOBE
The parietal lobes process sensory information, spatial orientation and awareness of the body in 3D space. Changes in activity here are linked to spiritual meditative experiences.

3 THALAMUS
The brain's sensory relay lights up during meditation as attention turns to specific sensations, like the feeling of the breath in the lungs.

4 FRONTAL LOBE
Activity in the large lobes at the front of the brain will increase as the meditator starts to consciously control the focus of their attention.

5 AMYGDALA
Activity in the brain's fear centre decreases. With prolonged meditation practice, this part of the brain may even shrink in size.

6 HIPPOCAMPUS
The part of the brain responsible for memory storage rewires in long-term meditators. The right hippocampus increases in size, affecting spatial memory and planning.

7 ANTERIOR CINGULATE CORTEX
Meditation increases grey matter in the part of the brain that handles attention allocation. This may aid focus and flexible thinking.

8 INSULA
Repeated meditation practice increases the connections inside the brain's internal sensation monitor, strengthening the brain's awareness of the body.

9 THOUGHT-FEAR CONNECTION
The link between the prefrontal cortex and the amygdala weakens with meditation practice, helping to stop fear and emotion interfering with attention and concentration.

at noticing when the mind starts to wander, and can learn to gently bring it back into focus. And, with experience, the default mode network actually starts to slow down.

A study of the brains of experienced versus novice meditators at Yale University found that repeated meditation practice re-tunes the default mode network. But rather than switch off, the network rewires. The connections in the network that control self-referencing and emotion weaken, while those involved in awareness of the present moment get stronger. This could explain why, in a meditative state, we are able to witness sensations, noticing the breath, the body or the thoughts without trying to interfere.

Losing your self in the moment

The yogic scholar Patanjali described meditation more as a state of mind than an activity. The practices of removing distraction, internalising the thoughts and focusing the attention all serve to bring the mind to a place where it can enter an effortless meditative state. In this state, known in Sanskrit as dhyana, the sense of self dissolves, and the senses of space and time also fall away.

This type of experience is one of the most challenging to study because it is hard to conjure up on demand, but scans of Tibetan Buddhist meditators revealed that it might be associated with a decrease in activity in the parietal lobes. These brain regions handle the processing involved in picturing the body in 3D space, working out what's you and what isn't, and keeping track of time. Changes here seem to have the power to alter our perception of ourselves, not only during meditation, but also following other powerful out-of-body or loss-of-self experiences. In another study, which asked nuns to relive past spiritual experiences, the parietal lobes also showed shifting patterns of activity.

Body-mind connection and your physical health

Meditation has obvious effects on the mind, but can also induce changes to the body. Our psychology is powerfully linked to our physiology. Mental stress floods the body with a trio of fight or flight hormones: adrenaline, noradrenaline and cortisol. Their role is to prepare us to fight, freeze or flee. They raise the heart rate, quicken breathing and alter the metabolism.

Addressing feelings of stress using meditation can change the state of the body by transitioning the mind out of its 'fight or flight' mode and into its opposite 'rest and digest'. It flips off the sympathetic nervous system, which governs the stress response, and flips on the parasympathetic nervous system, thereby easing the strain placed on the heart and lungs.

Studies examining meditation in people with anxiety, anger and high blood pressure have found that meditation not only makes people feel better, but it also reduces physical markers of stress. Stress hormones drop, inflammation markers fall, heart rate lowers, breathing slows down, and blood pressure decreases. For some, a single meditation session was enough to see a positive change.

Molecular studies suggest that the effects of meditation go deep into our physiology. In a small study at Harvard University, scientists found that 15 minutes of meditation every day for eight weeks could change patterns of gene expression. Our cells each carry an entire copy of the human genome, but they only need to use a handful of genes at any one time. So, they turn sets of genes on and off depending on what's happening around them. A regular meditation practice flipped the switch on 172 genes linked to the body clock, sugar metabolism and inflammation.

Beginning your own practice

Meditation is an active area of research and debate in the scientific community, and there is still much work to be done to understand how it affects the brain and how best to use it to improve health and wellbeing. But one of the best ways to learn more about the mental

> **MEDITATION MAKES PEOPLE FEEL BETTER, REDUCING PHYSICAL STRESS MARKERS**

and physical impact of a regular practice is to experience it for yourself.

It can be difficult to know where to begin, but although there are hundreds of techniques, they can all lead to the same tranquil state. It's just a case of finding the methods that work for you. A good place to start is guided meditation. Allowing someone else to take you through your practice – whether at a class, or via an app, video or podcast – can help to keep you focused when your mind starts to wander. And you don't have to commit to a long session. Research suggests that just a short period of regular training is enough for noticeable effects. Be consistent, start small, and build slowly.

Modern MEDITATION

Didn't think meditation was for you? You might think again once you've tried one of the many new ways to find your inner zen…

WORDS LOUISE PYNE

Meditation is nothing new. Humans have been paying attention to the breath and practising self-awareness for centuries, and for many years researchers have been exploring the benefits of meditation on both our physical wellbeing and our minds, with the body of scientific evidence steadily growing.

The list of benefits is pretty impressive. Slowing down racing thoughts has been shown to slash the risk of depression (or help treat it if you're already struggling with your mental health), by altering the release of mood-altering cytokines (inflammatory chemicals that are thought to lead to the development of chronic depression). It's also been shown to improve focus and attention, and help to beat insomnia.

"Meditation has been shown to reduce stress and anxiety, enhance self-awareness and increase the ability to self-regulate emotions. It helps you to get to know yourself, process what you are going through in life and puts some space between learned behaviours and knee jerk reactions," explains meditation expert and founder of Lunar Living, Kirsty Gallagher.

If traditional methods of meditation don't appeal, there are other meditation techniques that promise a chill fix. Here are some non-traditional ones you might want to try…

Walk your way to zen

Reconnecting with nature on a weekly basis helps to boost physical and mental wellbeing according to a recent study conducted by scientists at the University of Plymouth, and there's probably no better way to lower the stress scales than with a walking meditation. This involves bringing full presence and awareness into walking, something that many of us do all day every day without even thinking about it.

A separate study commissioned by the National Trust found that soaking up the sounds of nature relaxes us more than if we listen to a voiced meditation app, and results from tests showed that it reduced feelings of stress and anxiety by over a fifth. Connect with your senses on a mindful level »

> ❝ RECONNECTING WITH NATURE ON A WEEKLY BASIS HELPS TO BOOST PHYSICAL AND MENTAL WELLBEING ❞

MODERN MEDITATION

MANAGE YOUR MIND

109

to experience all that new seasons have to give, from crunching leaves, crackling fires and the pitter patter of a rainy day.

"Begin by simply standing and bringing your awareness into your body, where you feel the weight, how you're standing on the earth, bring full awareness and presence into your body. Then begin to walk slowly and feel each step mindfully. Put your awareness fully and completely into how it feels to be walking; fully experience the act of walking," shares Kirsty. Every time you notice your mind wandering, stop, bring your attention back into your body and begin walking again. Try to be truly present in that moment in the act of walking.

Harness the power of crystals

Semi-precious stones and crystals have been used for thousands of years to cure ailments and support emotional wellbeing. During the first lockdown of 2020, there was a surge in Google searches for 'healing crystals'. Crystal enthusiasts claim that these powerful gemstones hold energetic and healing frequencies that can be a helpful aid to meditation.

"For example, rose quartz will help amplify love, self-love, healing of the heart and energies of compassion and acceptance. Citrine will help with abundance and happiness. Amethyst will help bring calm and relaxing vibes, and something like black tourmaline will

3 MEDITATION TIPS FOR NEWBIES

1. MAKE A SCHEDULE
Try to set a meditation goal for two weeks or a whole month. Even if you feel like you won't have time, once you see the benefits you're likely to want to find the time to practise. Allocating roughly the same time for your practice each day will help with consistency.

2. KEEP A JOURNAL
Scribble down how you feel before and after each session. Even jotting down a short sentence or two will help you to keep track of how the sessions are helping you.

3. SET AN INTENTION
Not to be confused with a goal, an intention is something you want to align with in your life such as a purpose or attitude you'd like to commit to. Before each practice, set a specific intention to help focus your mind and heart. It could be to 'release fear' or 'to practise being kinder to yourself and to others', anything that is connected to your values and life principles.

> "THESE GEMSTONES HOLD ENERGETIC AND HEALING FREQUENCIES THAT CAN BE A HELPFUL AID"

help you to feel grounded and protected," claims Kirsty. "As you meditate with your crystal, it will emit these vibrations to you so that you can more easily begin to tune in to these things in yourself."

Some people find crystals useful as they provide a 'touchstone' through a meditation practice to help focus your intentions. "So, you can program your chosen crystal with what you would like to bring more of into your life and each time you sit and meditate with your crystal it will bring you back to your intention," Kirsty adds.

> ❝ SOUND BATHS ALTER THETA AND DELTA BRAIN WAVES, WHICH TRIGGER HEALING AND RELAXATION ❞

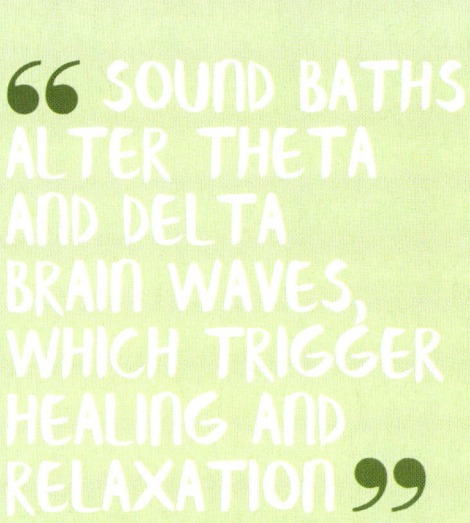

Boost sleep with beditation

With the pressure of work and family commitments, it can be a challenge to quieten your mind after a busy day so that you drift off to sleep. As many as 16 million of us suffer from poor sleep with a third confessing to insomnia according to one study by Aviva.

Sleep has a huge impact on long-term physical and mental wellbeing, and while how much we need per night varies from person to person, around seven to eight hours is the recommended amount.

A study published in *JAMA Internal Medicine* journal, which compared two groups of adults with sleeping troubles, found that practising a mindful meditation program was more effective at improving insomnia than a sleep education class that taught ways to improve sleep habits. And furthermore, if your goal is to improve sleep, practising meditation before hitting the hay (a technique called beditation) could possibly improve snoozing time more effectively than meditating during the day. "Beditation is the act of consciously releasing your day helping you to de-stress, relax and let go ready for a good night's sleep," explains Kirsty.

The great thing is that you can practise beditation from the comfort of your bed. "Close your eyes and take a few long, slow, deep breaths. Take a mental scan of your physical body and also how you feel energetically, mentally and emotionally. Notice anywhere that you feel tightness or as though you are gripping or holding on. This could be physical or emotional tension."

She goes on to add that with each long, slow, deep breath, simply let go.

"Feel as though you are processing and releasing your day ready for a restful sleep. Stay here for as long as you need to, simply exhaling and letting go until you feel a sense of becoming more relaxed and present."

Meditate to music

If sitting in silence doesn't do it, try a sound bath. This ancient therapy uses the sound of crystal singing bowls and chimes to ignite a relaxed, meditative state. Music makes us feel good, so it's no wonder that 88% of us turn to music when we need a boost.

Sound baths work by altering the theta and delta brain waves, which trigger healing and relaxation. All you have to do is lie back, get comfy and listen. Advocates maintain that the repetitive sounds and frequencies vibrate through your body creating a sense of peace.

Gaze at the moon

Celestial believers maintain that the lunar cycle affects our mood and energy levels, and we can tune in to its powers for guidance. "Usually we would use a new moon to meditate on what we want to create and bring into our lives and a full moon to do the work of releasing what we no longer need," believes Kirsty.

Living by lunar cycles is a centuries-old concept, but harnessing its purported mystical powers is something that we can bring into modern life, as Kirsty describes. "On the night of a new moon, make a list of your new moon intentions and what you would like to create in your life over the next lunar cycle. Then take a meditation where you visualise all of this coming easily and effortlessly to you. See yourself as though you already have all that you want and how that would feel. Sit in gratitude for all of your intentions coming true."

Once the full moon arrives, you can meditate under the moonlight. "Make a list of all that stands in your way and all you would like to let go of. Then lie on your back and begin to breathe slowly and deeply. With each deep exhale, feel as though you are gently breathing away anything that you no longer need. Feel yourself relax and surrender into the earth beneath you as you just let go with every breath," instructs Kirsty.

PUT PEN TO PAPER

PUT PEN

By giving ourselves space and time to practise journalling, we can often figure out what it is that is really bothering us

WORDS REBECCA LEWRY-GRAY

If you find mindfulness a tricky habit to develop, give journalling a try. In short you are writing down your thoughts and feelings in a mindful fashion, keeping an eye on your emotions and triggers. We can use journalling to reflect on our behaviours and solve anything that keeps reoccurring.

Why journal?
Journalling is on a par with meditation as you're tapping in to that deep part of your psyche that may be drowned out by the noisier distractions in our heads. You're giving yourself a quiet moment to 'be' and look inwards.

So many uses!
We can use journalling as a management tool for the stresses that modern life throws at us. Journals can be used to manage your workload and organise your thoughts and 'to dos', as well as calm yourself by dispassionately analysing your day. Journalling isn't just the preserve of teenagers in their bedrooms!

You're also training your brain by using both hemispheres of your brain at one time; the right side to feel creatively and the left side to work rationally.

There are so many different styles of journalling practice to try, so don't feel constrained to one – or if one type doesn't 'stick', start a new blank page and try again. Check out some of the options on the following pages. »

1 GRATITUDE JOURNAL

Gratitude journalling is a way of reflecting and taking stock of what you're thankful for in your life. These things can be life changing or minuscule in detail but it's important as you are essentially rewiring your viewpoint, by looking at your life in a positive way. If we think hard on the people and events in our life that we are grateful for, we may find ourselves becoming less materialistic – we're realising that the things we usually value (materially) aren't what make the world go round! Allow the gratitude you practise in your journal to spill into your life.

2 PROMPTED JOURNALS

If the idea of a blank page fills you with dread, help is at hand. Journalling has become very popular over recent years, and prompted journals are a great place to start for many people. These journals guide you through the process, and can keep you accountable and focused. The wide range of prompted journals also cater for many specific types and kinds of journal-ers – from teens to people looking to be more mindful. There is no standard prompted journal, as the 'right' choice for you may not be the same for everyone. Keep in mind what you want to get out of journalling when looking for a prompted journal. Take a look at reviews to check the tone and commitment level before you buy.

3 DREAM JOURNAL

Dreaming is a bit like unconscious mindfulness – our brains process our past in a subjective way, filing it away. Annoyingly, we often forget our dreams when we wake up. Writing a dream journal can improve our dream memory skills, and you may find that your dream memory becomes stronger after a period of dream journalling. Try to write your dreams down as soon as you wake up to catch all the details. You can then use a dream dictionary to find reoccurring themes or try to work out your own personal meanings.

4 FAMILY JOURNAL

Family journalling is essentially sharing your journal and writing with other members of your family. You take turns writing in the journal, talking about things you may struggle to address in person. Do this mindfully, keeping an eye on your intentions – you're not looking to start a fight. You and your family members are opening yourselves up to each other and perspectives can change, depending on the viewpoint of others. Family journals can be very interesting with children, who may struggle to express themselves eloquently. When you focus your writing with other people, you're practising empathy, which can only be a good thing.

5 BULLET JOURNAL

A bullet journal, on first inspection, often looks like a confusing mix of shorthand and symbols. Essentially, bullet journalling is rapid logging. You're capturing everything you need to in bulleted lists and this can be incredibly useful for planning and logging important tasks (less so for personal introspection). Tasks, events and notes are symbolised by dots, circles and dashes respectively. You can use your own method, such as using asterisks to signify importance, or exclamation marks to show great ideas or things you don't want to forget. Bullet journalling is an incredibly efficient way to get all your thoughts down on paper, and as a reminder to action your ideas!

6 ART JOURNAL

Journalling doesn't have to take the form of a handwriting-heavy tome. If you are a visual person or a creative one at that, an art journal may be the best way for you to begin your journalling journey. Try to include your sketches, experiments and reflections on how a task turned out – whether this is a piece of art or a day-to-day task. Play with your journal; often we can articulate

> "PROMPTED JOURNALS GUIDE YOU THROUGH THE PROCESS, AND KEEP YOU ACCOUNTABLE AND FOCUSED"

ourselves better through mark-making and art than through words. It's important to get pen (or pencil/crayon/paint) to paper and make that first mark, and not get too hung up on perfection – this journal is just for you – you don't have to let anyone else in.

FREE WRITING

Spill your thoughts out onto your page. Free writing is quite different to the other types of journalling on this list. While journals such as dream journals, bullet journals and planning journals work due to their structure, free writing is more free (the clue is in the name). Think of it like a brain dump or stream-of-consciousness writing. Try not to edit yourself and you may find you're getting into the nitty gritty of what you're really concerned about. Use this kind of journalling consciously. Instead of feeling like it's yet another thing to do on your list of jobs, enjoy the task. Focus on your 'why' of journalling and keep yourself in the present moment while writing.

PLANNING JOURNAL

Whether you consider yourself a 'planner' or not, a planning journal is a great investment in your mental health. Everyone can miss things off the to-do list or fail to hit a deadline. You can use planning journals for short- to medium-term planning in home life as well as work. This kind of journal can help you develop the habit of planning – and can assist in goal-setting too. If you find your day gets eaten up by constantly checking emails and addressing things as they come in, you can find security in organising your day hour-by-hour to ensure your tasks are completed.

SPIRITUAL JOURNALS

If you are a spiritual or religious person, you can use a journal to help you explore this more fully. You can use this kind of journal to carve out time in your day for this kind of focus and track your growth. Pick a daily reflection and work on it in your journal.

TIME CAPSULE

Journalling can have a finite timeline. You may wish to journal about a very specific part of your life, whether positive or negative. You may also wish to journal about current events – we live in interesting times and by including clippings and collages, you can create a full picture of what life is like.

POSITIVITY JOURNAL

Try to use your journalling time to reflect on the positive things in your life. Similar to gratitude-journalling, when we consciously look at what we have in our lives, we often find there is a lot to be happy about. When things go wrong in life it is important to look for the silver linings. Sometimes this is easier said than done, but try to remember the power of positive thinking.

HOBBY JOURNAL

If you are the kind of person who always has a project on the go, a hobby journal might be a great fit for you. You will be able to track progress on larger projects, and also collate and brainstorm inspiration for future projects. If you are working on a hobby that has a clear path of improvement, you are then able to set goals for what you would like to achieve and then use the previous entries to see how far you have come. Many avid readers use journals to track must-read books, as well as review and manage the pile of books they have on their bedside table. If you're a gardener, this kind of reflection is handy for noting the changes we see in our gardens and tracking the journey that nature has close to home.

QUICK JOURNAL

If you feel like regular journalling is too much of a time sink for you, give quick journalling a try. It's simple – write one sentence a day. That's it! While this may sound simple, it's an incredibly interesting exercise, as you are editing your memories of your day and working out what is truly important – what is valuable to record and reflect on? Keep this habit for as long as you can and you may find the routine sticks and you extend your entries. Your journal may evolve and change during your time writing – there's no rule to say you must stick to one type.

LET THE TREES *Treat You*

From boosting mood to immunity, forest bathing is fantastic for improving our wellbeing. Grab your coat, get outside and enjoy the wonders of woodland

WORDS SARA NIVEN

We know fresh air is good for us and natural surroundings are an obvious choice for getting that, but while the coast can be calming, it is a well-established fact that wooded areas and forests are the most powerful places when it comes to restorative effects.

The idea of forest bathing, or Shinrin-yoku as it is known in Japan, where the idea first originated in the 1980s, has become increasingly popular and is supported by professionals in both medical and psychological fields.

"With over half the world's population now living in urban areas, we have become more removed from nature, but numerous studies show the mental health benefits of reconnecting, specifically by immersing yourself in a forest or woodland atmosphere," confirms Professor Stephen Palmer, founder director of both the International Centre for Ecopsychology and also the Centre for Stress Management. "Overall, forest bathing induces relaxation and enhances wellbeing while research has found specific reductions in levels of anxiety, depression, stress and even selfishness."

Come to your senses
To get the most from an experience and truly 'bathe', Professor Palmer explains that you should use all your senses – sight, smell, touch, hearing and, if safe to do so, taste. (The latter should only ever be undertaken with expert, professional guidance if tasting plants.)

To prevent distractions if walking with your friends and family, he advises staying a safe distance apart and avoiding conversation. Give each other plenty of space and it is best to turn your mobile phone off too. Then try these suggestions:

Walk slowly through the forest or wood, avoiding rushing. Listen to the sound of your footsteps. Take the opportunity to stop and look all around you. If you go at different times of the day, you will notice changes in the light. Your experience will also vary depending on the seasons.

On your next forest bathing session, when you stop, listen to the birdsong. Focus on a particular bird. Look up at the tree canopy.

On your following trip, you may wish to take a rug with you for this exercise. In the forest, assuming that it is safe to do so, find a flat area where you can lay down and gaze upwards. Look at the leaves. Notice the different shades of green. You may notice that you have started to relax. If so, slowly breathe in and out and taste the freshness of the air. Become aware of the natural wood fragrance found in forests.

On another occasion, softly touch a tree with your fingers, then with the palm of your hand. Reflect on what you notice. Smell the bark of the tree. Appreciate the time it has taken the tree to grow.

Forest bathing benefits
Forest bathing can boost your mood. It's been shown to help reduce negative emotions such as anger and fear, while increasing feelings of happiness and general wellbeing. Inje University in Seoul, South Korea, carried out a study of patients with major depressive disorder, treating some in a forest environment and others in hospital. Results showed that the four-week forest programme improved the patients' depressive symptoms and generated remission in patients taking medication for at least three months.

Incredibly, the physical benefits of forest bathing don't stop there. It can also improve your immune system and reduce levels of stress-related hormones such as cortisol and adrenaline. Western studies have tended to focus on the visual and, to a secondary extent, the auditory impact of forest environments. However, Shinrin-yoku also places an emphasis on smell. Dr Qing Li, a leading forest bathing expert, immunologist and author of *Into The Forest: How Trees Can Help You Find Health And Happiness*, reports that when people walk through a forest, they inhale organic compounds called phytoncides. These compounds actively boost our immune system and have even been studied for anti-cancer properties.

LET THE TREES TREAT YOU

Forest bathing has also been known to make us kinder to ourselves, and others. Recent research by Yasuhiro Kotera and Dean Fido reported an increase in self-compassion, common humanity and mindfulness in students who participated in a three-day Shinrin-yoku retreat in Fukushima.

Other field studies have confirmed that time spent in nature improves our connection with others. Research by the University of Illinois revealed that residents in city public housing who were surrounded by greenery felt a stronger bond with neighbours than tenants in buildings without trees, and they also felt safer and better adjusted to their environment. There was a reduced risk of street crime and lower levels of aggression between domestic partners. The residents with trees reported using "more constructive, less violent ways of dealing with conflicts."

So what are you waiting for? Head for the forest! Your body and mind will thank you.

BRING THE OUTDOORS IN

Even when indoors, you can still experience some of the benefits that forest bathing and nature provide. A study in the *Journal of Physiological Anthropology* shows that simply touching and smelling indoor plants can lower stress levels, while a US study of patients recovering after surgery found that those staying in rooms overlooking trees were able to leave hospital sooner than those with views of a brick wall. Berlin-based artist Libby Page specialises in large-scale paintings of trees, including forest scenes and canopies, and says clients often tell her they notice their mood improves after hanging her art.

"I choose to paint trees and woodland scenes because I personally find them very relaxing and am aware of research showing that even looking at pictures of them can be beneficial," she says. "I like to think my pictures bring some of the benefits of forest bathing into people's homes."

> **FOREST BATHING INDUCES RELAXATION AND ENHANCES WELLBEING**

EMBRACE THE *Blue*

Could spending time near water be the key to feeling healthier and happier?

EMBRACE THE BLUE

WORDS ALI HORSFALL

If you've ever fallen asleep to the sound of the sea or been brave enough to take an invigorating, wild skinny-dip, you can't deny the positive effects of being in and around water. The ancient Greeks soaked in mineral-rich thermal springs to help them feel better, and seaside trips were often prescribed by doctors during Victorian times. And it seems they were on to something, because now there's a body of science-led evidence to prove that water can indeed heal. Keen to learn more? Here's how to ride the wave of 'blue therapy'.

Join the blue gym
The great outdoors is a healthy place to relax and recharge, as many of us discovered when embracing the goodness of green spaces during the pandemic. But along with fields, forests and our favourite parks, natural water is an element of mother nature that offers similar wellbeing benefits. "The term 'blue space' is used to refer to our oceans, seas, rivers, lakes, ponds, streams and waterfalls – but can actually include all kinds of water, and research is increasingly showing how these watery spaces can help us physically and psychologically," explains Dr Catherine Kelly, geography academic and author of *Blue Spaces: How & Why Water Can Make You Feel Better* (£14.99 ($17.50), Welbeck).

The concept of spending time in blue space was introduced over a decade ago in the UK as an initiative by the Department of Health and Peninsula Medical School in Plymouth, and it's since been championed by wellness experts and water-lovers as a very valid way to feel good. The overarching idea is that coastal and natural water environments – dubbed the 'blue gym' – can be used specifically to increase physical »

> " COASTAL AND NATURAL WATER ENVIRONMENTS CAN BE USED TO INCREASE PHYSICAL ACTIVITY AND REDUCE STRESS "

EMBRACE THE BLUE

activity, reduce stress and build stronger communities. One study[1] found that living near blue spaces, visiting them, or even just enjoying a nice waterscape view, is associated with a lower risk of depression, anxiety and other mental health disorders, as well as encouraging relaxation.

A space to switch off
Ocean advocate Lizzi Larbalestier says she feels deeply attached to the Cornish coastline, where she lives and works as a blue health coach – helping others discover the wellbeing benefits of the sea (goingcoastal. blue). "I see people arrive anxious and stressed by the daily pressures of city life and the digital world. Stepping into blue space enables them to slow down, breathe and awaken their senses, connecting with a wider, more analogue world that has light, shade, colour and form," she says.

The environment proves to be the perfect antidote to time-pressured, device-driven lifestyles. "Blue space is a sensory landscape, meaning we engage all of our senses when we are in it," says Catherine Kelly. "We hear the sounds of the water ebbing and flowing, we notice the colours of the sea or stream, we can feel the sandy beach beneath our toes, smell the sea air or the wildflowers along a canal bank, and we can taste the salt on our skin after a dip in the ocean."

The outcome is positive. Busy minds will quieten without effort and it's possible to have tangible and tactile experiences that are not mediated by technology. "Water is medicine and in our fast-paced world, the sense of peace and presence it provides is undervalued and underutilised," says Lizzi. "You soon realise that we are part of an ecosystem, far from being disconnected and isolated, and that we each have a contribution to make."

Body benefits of blue
Research reveals that spending time by water also encourages us to be more active, whether that's surfing the waves or having a riverside stroll. "We then get all the physical benefits associated with exercise, such as improved cardiovascular health, combating osteoporosis and endorphin releases.

> "BEING NEXT TO A LARGE BODY OF NATURAL WATER INSPIRES A SENSE OF AWE. GAZING AT THE HORIZON GIVES A SENSE OF PERSPECTIVE ON DAILY LIFE"

EMBRACE THE BLUE

Plus, the happy hormones, serotonin and dopamine, rise when moving on, in or near water," says Catherine. Tempted to take a dip? Studies show that swimming in natural water may help with anxiety and depression, digestive issues and menopause symptoms. "Cold-water swimming stimulates the vagus nerve in the body, and this can induce an anti-inflammatory response, which researchers are linking to improved health," says Catherine. Visit outdoorswimmingsociety.com for tips on doing it safely.

Water for mental wellness
There's a biological reason why respite and reflection become possible in blue spaces. "Levels of the stress hormones adrenaline and cortisol in the body can drop, breathing regulates and the heart rate slows, so in essence we feel calmer and our mood improves," says Catherine. In this blue mind state, it's easier to practise mindfulness – water's meditative quality brings us into the present moment and allows us to press pause on our worries. "Being next to a large body of natural water inspires a sense of awe. Gazing at the horizon gives a sense of perspective on daily life and there's a feeling of being part of something bigger," says Catherine.

5 WAYS TO SOAK UP BLUE SPACE

Get the feel-good benefits of water with these easy ideas to work into your day

1. SWITCH UP YOUR WALKS
Blue space walking is a simple way you can connect with water. "Check an online map to find your nearest water sources such as a river, lake or canal, and factor them into your weekly walks," says Catherine.

2. SOOTHE WITH SOUNDS
Listening to water inspires calmness, focus and creativity. Even the smallest garden or balcony has room for a battery-powered water feature, or download an app that has sounds of the ocean. Try Naturespace (free on App Store and Google Play).

3. HAVE A RESTORATIVE BATH
A relaxing dunk in the tub will deliver benefits, says Catherine. Add healing minerals that are found in seawater.

4. TAKE AN ENERGISING SHOWER
As advocated by Wim Hof, aka The Ice Man, turn your shower to cold for an invigorating blast that will stimulate anti-inflammatory action in the body. "Start with 30 seconds for a few days, then build up to one minute, until you can handle two or three minutes of completely cold water," says Catherine.

5. ENJOY A WATER-BASED HOBBY
You don't have to sail, surf or swim to have fun around water. Try stand-up paddleboarding (SUP) – you can do this on lakes and canals. Sketch or paint a sea view, or take regular bike rides along a blue route.

Not near the sea? Get a city fix
Urbanites can still seek refuge in blue space. "In towns and cities, you can walk by a river or canal on the way to work, or find an outdoor fountain to sit by as you eat lunch," suggests Catherine. "If you deliberately notice the sight and sounds of moving water, you'll learn to tune out other stimuli. Focus on relaxing your breathing and enjoy a moment of peace." Many cities also have great outdoor lidos, which offer the 'fresh-air experience' while boosting social and physical wellbeing.

> **SWIMMING IN NATURAL WATER MAY HELP WITH ANXIETY AND DEPRESSION, AND MENOPAUSE SYMPTOMS**

[1] International Journal of Hygiene and Environmental Health

COULD COLOUR BE THE CURE?

COULD *Colour* BE THE CURE?

Discover how immersing yourself in the right tones can work wonders for your wellbeing

WORDS FAYE M. SMITH

Do you often have more confidence when wearing a certain shade, or feel more positive after walking in green spaces? It could be that colour is having a much bigger effect on your wellbeing then you realise.

"Colour is a quintessential part of life," says colour specialist Mark Wentworth (colourforlife.com). "Each colour creates a different physical and emotional response and, as we have evolved as a species, so has our understanding of the depths and intricacies of human emotion and behaviour."

But how we respond to the effects of certain hues, whether positively or negatively, can be very personal – there isn't a one-colour-fits-all when it comes to colour therapy. "On one level, colour is instinctual, and on another it connects us to our own personal memories and experiences," explains Wentworth. "Most people love something, such as sky blue, as it has an overall calming effect, maybe it reminds us of summer holidays and times of carefree daydreaming, and yet for some it's depressing, cold and detached." Hertfordshire University fashion psychologist Professor Karen Pine, working with Comfort UK, agrees: "We may love or hate the colour of our old school uniform, for example, depending on whether we have strong positive or negative memories of school."

With such personal responses to colour, there might be some trial and error when finding what's right for you, before you reap the benefits. "Be brave, experiment," says Wentworth. "Learn to understand your own colour language and how it reflects the highs and lows of your life story. Love your colours and watch your life transform." Here's how...

A wardrobe of personality

Whether you're dedicated to fashion or not, the colour of your clothing can have a significant impact on your mental health. You don't have to go head to toe – just a pop of colour will work, which is good news, as 34%[1] of women are scared to change the way they look. "Dressing for how you feel promotes an overall confidence and authenticity, which creates a positive approach from other people,"

> ❝ DRESSING FOR HOW YOU FEEL PROMOTES CONFIDENCE ❞

MANAGE YOUR MIND

COULD COLOUR BE THE CURE?

says Wentworth. "If you have a goal, you can booby-trap your wardrobe with colour to attract what you want." He suggests the following...

YELLOW
is sunshine, brightness and fun. There'll never be a dull moment when you're wearing yellow.

PURPLE
says 'I am my own person and I'll stand out from the crowd'. Wearing it inspires creativity and commands respect.

BLUE
conveys trust and openness. We'd probably sit down and share our hopes and dreams with someone wearing blue, as blue overall tends to make us feel safe, whatever the shade.

GREEN
brings freshness and the impression that everything will happen in its own good time. When we wear green, we offer a level-headed approach to life.

BLACK
is sophistication and elegance – it adds style and class due to its ability to highlight everything else around it. It makes other colours appear bolder and stronger, and it conveys mystery.

Love a PATTERN?
You'll still benefit from the colours, but mixing them can dilute the effects, as intricate or repetitive detailing can pull focus.

Worried about wearing red?
Although a lot of people talk about feeling brave when wearing red, it can have negative connotations. "According to a study, men thought women were more interested in sex if they wore a red rather than a white T-shirt," says Professor Pine. "Evolutionary psychologists have shown that men ask women more intimate questions if they are wearing red. Women rate men who wear red as being more attractive."

Blondes really do have more fun
Feel more positive after a trip to the salon? You're not alone. A study by Nottingham Trent University and Clairol found that women who dyed their hair blonde had increased levels of confidence. It's thought that a strong and bold hair colour is similar to what we had as children, and therefore exudes a feeling of youthfulness. "Colouring your hair may seem like an art to most people, but there is actually a lot of science behind it," says Dr Mark Sergeant, who led

DID YOU KNOW?

Many banks use the colour blue in their logos, as do Facebook, LinkedIn and X, because it helps companies seem trustworthy.

....

64% of Brits believe how they dress can make them feel better about themselves and boost their mood, says a study by Comfort UK.
Comfort UK's white paper, Long Live Clothes

....

A shade of pink called Baker-Miller has been used to reduce violence in hostile environments, due to the colour's calming properties.

COULD COLOUR BE THE CURE?

> "ALTHOUGH A LOT OF PEOPLE TALK ABOUT FEELING BRAVE WHEN WEARING RED, IT CAN HAVE NEGATIVE CONNOTATIONS"

the research. "Not only were their confidence and mood levels elevated, but many reported feeling more attractive and sexually exciting."

Colour in the home
When it comes to the walls or decorations at home, following the trends can be a bad idea. "We should be wary of doing so when painting in our homes," says Professor Pine. "Our environment is an expression of our individuality – it needs to resonate with our emotions and provide a haven to return to. We will feel more at home in a colour scheme that chimes with our personality than one dictated by a trend." Don't have the same taste as your partner? "Choosing colours can be a minefield for couples so agree at the start that you may need to compromise," says expert Georgina Burnett, from **homeimprovementmonth.co.uk**. "If you like orange and he/she isn't keen, maybe this needs to be an accent colour in the room, against something more neutral like grey."

Boost your sex life
The colour of your bedroom walls and bedding could make a difference in how much sex you have each week, found a survey by **littlewoods.com**...

- Purple – 3.49 times
- Red – 3.18 times
- Sky blue – 3.14 times
- Pink – 3.02 times
- Black – 2.99 times
- Grey – 1.8 times

Green, beige and white are best avoided. "Dark green is a stop sign," says Georgina.

Kitchen overhaul
Had the same set of crockery for years? The colour of your plates could affect how you eat…

If you're caring for someone with health issues, avoid serving food on white plates. "They are the worst colour for hospitals," says professor of experimental psychology Dr Charles Spence. "With dementia or visual problems, there may not be enough of a contrast between the food and the white plate, so you want the food to stand out against a coloured plate."

Don't want to add extra spice? University of Valencia scientists found that those who ate from a white plate found food 13% more flavourful.

Researchers from the University of Oxford have discovered that if you eat from a red plate, you will eat less. "What you serve food on turns out to have more of an impact on our taste and flavour perception than any of us realise," says Dr Spence. "You end up eating a little bit less because red on a plate seems to trigger some sort of avoidance signal."

Flower power
The right colourful bouquet of blooms can help give a much-needed boost. "It's no accident that we buy people flowers to cheer them up or to express our love," says Professor Pine. "The attractive and fragrant colours produced by nature have an uplifting effect on our emotions." Not sure what to pick? "Yellow chrysanthemums are perfect for someone facing a new challenge," says floral designer Lara Sanjar, working with **funnyhowflowersdothat.co.uk**. "While purple anemones can help to keep you inspired for creative projects."

Immerse yourself outside
During the summer months, it's worth swapping the treadmill for walking outdoors in fields or woodlands. Experts at the University of Essex found that doing any exercise outside can boost your mood in just five minutes. "People have been soaking up the healing power of nature for centuries, but it is only in recent years that scientists have produced peer-reviewed evidence that there are measurable benefits to our bodies when we spend time among the trees," explains Beth Kempton, author of *Wabi Sabi: Japanese Wisdom for a Perfectly Imperfect Life* (Piatkus, £16.99). "These include increased mental wellness; boosted immune systems; and reduced stress levels, heart rate and blood pressure, which has led to the concept of 'shinrin-yoku' (forest bathing) being recognised as a kind of therapy."

---

1. Mark Wentworth is working with Valspar's Love Your Colour Guarantee. It lets you change your mind about paint colour – if you don't love your first choice, Valspar will swap it completely free of charge.

WHICH *therapy* IS FOR ME?

There's a multitude of problems therapy can help with and just as many approaches to take. How do you know which is right for you?

▸ WHICH THERAPY IS FOR ME? ◂

WORDS SARA NIVEN

PSYCHODYNAMIC PSYCHOTHERAPY

Stemming from Sigmund Freud's psychoanalysis, Freud believed that psychological problems are rooted in the unconscious mind, and experiences from a person's past can influence their thoughts and behaviour in later life. Positive change is seen as happening as a result of uncovering repressed events and linking them to present difficulties. You might spend significant time discussing your childhood or recalling dreams, with your therapist suggesting connections. This approach also emphasises the idea and exploration of transference, where feelings you experienced in previous relationships may be projected onto your therapist – for example, you view them as a critical teacher or favourite uncle.
Suitable for A wide range of issues, including depression and anxiety.
Considerations Some people might prefer to focus on the present than revisit their childhood. Therapy may take place over a longer time frame than some other approaches.

PERSON-CENTRED THERAPY

This form of therapy falls into a category called 'humanistic', where the client is seen as able to solve difficulties themselves, given the right conditions. Developed by psychologist Carl Rogers in the 1940s, there is an emphasis on the counsellor showing unconditional positive regard (UPR), which refers to non-judgemental warmth and acceptance. The therapist aims to ensure a client feels heard and understood, and enables them to lead the session and set the pace. Compared to a psychodynamic counsellor, a person-centred one is more likely to occasionally reveal their own experiences (self-disclosure) if they see it as helpful for emphasising understanding.
Suitable for All ages and a wide range of issues, including grief, depression, anxiety and stress.
Considerations The outcome of person-centred therapy depends on what a client chooses to talk about in sessions. Some people might want more directive help than this form of counselling typically provides.

GESTALT THERAPY

Gestalt therapy is another form of humanistic therapy based on the belief in a client's natural ability to achieve healthy balance and growth. Developed by psychotherapists Fritz and Laura Perls, it places a strong focus on immediacy in addition to the client/counsellor relationship.
Although any skilled therapist will pay attention to your body language, a Gestalt therapist is more likely to comment on this. They might tell you they notice you tapping your feet when discussing a particular topic, for instance, and encourage you to »

> "SOME PREFER TO FOCUS ON THE PRESENT THAN REVISIT CHILDHOOD"

MANAGE YOUR MIND

WHICH THERAPY IS FOR ME?

> "A CBT THERAPIST WILL BE MORE DIRECTIVE AND ENCOURAGE YOU TO CHALLENGE NEGATIVE BELIEFS"

consider what that means. There might also be aspects of role playing and creativity, using pebbles or other objects. The 'empty chair' is a well-known Gestalt technique where a client is encouraged to address a chair as though someone they have an unresolved issue with is sitting there.
Suitable for Issues including anxiety, depression, low self-esteem and relationship problems.
Considerations Some people enjoy the more creative techniques used in Gestalt therapy, while others might feel uncomfortable. As with any form of counselling, feeling safe and having a good level of trust with your therapist is key.

COGNITIVE BEHAVIOURAL THERAPY (CBT)

CBT falls under the category of behavioural therapy and is goal orientated. A CBT therapist will be more directive and encourage you to challenge and change negative or outdated beliefs that are causing difficulties. They might also set 'homework' to do between sessions.

This could be a good approach for conquering a specific fear, such as starting to drive again after a road accident. While a person-centred counsellor would focus on empathy and understanding, a CBT therapist would be aiming to uncover the beliefs and fears you have about this, challenge these and take steps towards overcoming them.
Suitable for In addition to depression and anxiety, CBT can be used to treat obsessive compulsive disorder (OCD), phobias and substance abuse issues.

Considerations Therapy tends to be focused on specific goals and outcomes and is often relatively short term. Exposure therapy (where you confront situations you generally avoid) can be challenging.

DIALECTICAL BEHAVIOURAL THERAPY (DBT)

An adaptation of CBT, which uses some of the same skills, DBT was developed in the 1970s and is aimed at people who struggle with very intense emotions. For this reason, it is the therapy of choice for treating people diagnosed with borderline personality disorder (BPD). Like CBT, it focuses on change but there is more of an emphasis on mindfulness and learning how to regulate emotions and tolerate distress without turning to harmful coping mechanisms.
Suitable for Mental health conditions, including BPD, self-harm, eating issues, addiction and PTSD.
Considerations People undergoing DBT might be asked to commit to more than just one-to-one sessions – group skills training, phone coaching and homework could also be involved.

TRANSACTIONAL ANALYSIS (TA)

Transactional analysis focuses on the way you relate to others, be that your partner, your boss or a family member. Developed by psychiatrist Eric Berne in the late 1950s, it divides the human personality into three basic ego states: parent (with nurturing and critical sides), adult and child. This aims to increase our understanding of interacting with others and the responses we get, such as regularly being in critical parent mode when speaking to your partner, which then results in conflict.

TA therapists also look at our beliefs in terms of 'scripts' and help a client re-evaluate any unhelpful ones formed while growing up, which are impacting negatively on them, for example, 'I must never make a mistake'.
Suitable for A range of issues, including relationship difficulties, low self-esteem and workplace challenges. TA is often applied outside of the therapy room, for example in coaching or educational situations.
Considerations Supporters of TA cite the simple models and language, which are much easier than some other theories for clients to understand and apply to everyday situations.

EYE MOVEMENT DESENSITISATION REPROCESSING THERAPY (EMDR)

Developed by a psychologist called Francine Shapiro in the late 1980s, EMDR aims to help the brain to reprocess traumatic memories. Clients won't lose the memory but ideally it should not continue to trigger such strong emotions.

EMDR has a specific structure, with eight stages that a therapist works through with you. After the initial stages, therapy involves activating a disturbing memory while introducing what is called bilateral stimulation (BLS) involving eye movements, physical tapping or other stimuli to activate both sides of the brain.
Suitable for EMDR is recognised by the World Health Organization (WHO) as a treatment for post-traumatic stress disorder (PTSD). It can also be used for a range of other issues, such as unresolved grief and mental illnesses, including personality disorders.
Considerations Talking about difficult memories in detail isn't seen as a significant part of the process, which could be helpful for people keen to avoid that, although they will be asked to recall experiences. This therapy isn't considered suitable for clients with substance abuse issues.

ART THERAPY

As the name suggests, this form of psychotherapy uses art as a form of communication and way of addressing difficult emotions. Complex emotions can be put onto paper or canvas, and creating and discussing the resulting art with a therapist can help give clients clarity over intense but confused feelings and connect with their unconscious mind.
Suitable for Art therapy can be used by people in a wide range of situations, including physical illnesses, such as cancer, learning disabilities, eating disorders and dementia. It can also be used with children.
Considerations You don't need to be a budding Michelangelo or Monet to have art therapy – no artistic skills are necessary; however, some people may feel less comfortable than others expressing themselves in this way. A skilled therapist should provide plenty of opportunity to work through the emotions the art session brings up.

INTEGRATIVE THERAPY

Rather than specialising in one, many therapists now train in a range of different therapeutic approaches and use these like tools in a toolbox, to be taken out according to what seems most useful at the time. One week they might work in an entirely person-centred way, allowing the client to lead the session. Another time, they might outline the ego states that are part of TA theory to help the client gain insight into a relationship difficulty, or draw on Gestalt training to suggest the 'empty chair' exercise.
Suitable for Integrative therapy is increasingly common and seen as suitable for many issues including bereavement, relationship difficulties and eating disorders.
Considerations This is a more 'bespoke,' form of therapy with less structure than some others, but shouldn't be experienced as confusing or completely random. Integrative therapists work to tailor their approach to a client's needs, not use different ones just for the sake of variety.

HYPNOTHERAPY

Hypnotherapy isn't a theoretical approach or considered a traditional talking therapy that falls under the remit of the British Association of Counselling and Psychotherapy or the American Counseling Association.

However, there is evidence that it can be an effective form of treatment for anxiety and anxiety-related disorders, such as headaches and irritable bowel syndrome, while others report finding it helpful in addressing a range of other difficulties.

During sessions, hypnosis combined with talking therapy aims to work on both a conscious and subconscious level, to bring about positive change while adjustments can be made to limiting beliefs that have influenced or directed the client's life.
Suitable for Anxiety, phobias, addictions, low self-esteem, insomnia and stress-related conditions.
Considerations Hypnotherapy isn't advised if you have psychosis or a personality disorder. As with any form of therapy, it is important to ensure a hypnotherapist is suitably trained and check them out with the relevant regulatory body.

Whatever therapy you opt for, it is essential your therapist is properly qualified and works to professional standards. In the UK, the best way to establish this is via the **British Association for Counselling and Psychotherapy (BACP)** *(www.bacp.co.uk/about-therapy/how-to-find-a-therapist)*, and in the US, the **American Counseling Association (ACA)**. *(www.counseling.org/aca-community/learn-about-counseling/what-is-counseling/find-a-counselor)*

Manage Your Mind

BUILD A BETTER RELATIONSHIP WITH YOUR MIND TODAY

Future PLC Quay House, The Ambury, Bath, BA1 1UA

Editorial
Group Editor **Sarah Bankes**
Art Editor **Madelene King**
Head of Art & Design **Greg Whitaker**
Editorial Director **Jon White**
Managing Director **Grainne McKenna**

Contributors
Julie Bassett, Scott Dutfield, Rose Goodman, Ailsa Harvey, Ali Horsfall, Trisha Lewis, Rebecca Lewry-Gray, Natalia Lubomirski, Laura Mears, Alison Morgan, Sara Niven, Louise Pyne, Jenny Rowe, Faye M Smith, Debra Waters, Samantha Wood

Photography
All copyrights and trademarks are recognised and respected

Advertising
Media packs are available on request
Commercial Director **Clare Dove**

International
Head of Print Licensing **Rachel Shaw**
licensing@futurenet.com
www.futurecontenthub.com

Circulation
Head of Newstrade **Tim Mathers**

Production
Head of Production **Mark Constance**
Production Project Manager **Matthew Eglinton**
Advertising Production Manager **Joanne Crosby**
Digital Editions Controller **Jason Hudson**
Production Managers **Keely Miller, Nola Cokely, Vivienne Calvert, Fran Twentyman**

Printed in the UK

Distributed by Marketforce – www.marketforce.co.uk
For enquiries, please email: mfcommunications@futurenet.com

Manage Your Mind First Edition (LBZ6398)
© 2024 Future Publishing Limited

We are committed to only using magazine paper which is derived from responsibly managed, certified forestry and chlorine-free manufacture. The paper in this bookazine was sourced and produced from sustainable managed forests, conforming to strict environmental and socioeconomic standards.

All contents © 2024 Future Publishing Limited or published under licence. All rights reserved. No part of this magazine may be used, stored, transmitted or reproduced in any way without the prior written permission of the publisher. Future Publishing Limited (company number 2008885) is registered in England and Wales. Registered office: Quay House, The Ambury, Bath BA1 1UA. All information contained in this publication is for information only and is, as far as we are aware, correct at the time of going to press. Future cannot accept any responsibility for errors or inaccuracies in such information. You are advised to contact manufacturers and retailers directly with regard to the price of products/services referred to in this publication. Apps and websites mentioned in this publication are not under our control. We are not responsible for their contents or any other changes or updates to them. This magazine is fully independent and not affiliated in any way with the companies mentioned herein.

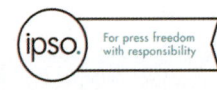

FUTURE
Connectors. Creators. Experience Makers.

Future plc is a public company quoted on the London Stock Exchange (symbol: FUTR)
www.futureplc.com

Chief Executive Officer **Jon Steinberg**
Non-Executive Chairman **Richard Huntingford**
Chief Financial Officer **Sharjeel Suleman**

Tel +44 (0)1225 442 244